D0807023

IN SEARCH OF MY TRUE IDENTITY

A Journey from Disillusionment and Despair
to Hope and Fulfillment

Suzanne H. Fabbi, M.Ed.

BALBOA
PRESS

A DIVISION OF HAY HOUSE

Balboa Press books may be ordered through booksellers or by contacting:

Balboa Press
A Division of Hay House
1663 Liberty Drive
Bloomington, IN 47403
www.balboapress.com
1 (877) 407-4847

Print information available on the last page.

ISBN: 978-1-9822-2746-3 (sc)
ISBN: 978-1-9822-2745-6 (hc)
ISBN: 978-1-9822-2751-7 (e)

Balboa Press rev. date: 05/01/2019

Dedicated to my two mothers and to my fathers up
above, who have always kept me in their care.
To my four children—may you never
doubt the love of your mother.
To my husband, who has held my hand on the journey.

CONTENTS

Part III: Truth Revealed

PROLOGUE

At sixty-two years old, a wife for nearly forty-five years, a mother of four grown and accomplished children, a grandmother of seven incredibly talented grandchildren, and a retired secondary English teacher by profession, I sit here editing the story of my beginnings. Ever since I found my birth family, I have talked of writing a book about my adoption. I wonder if anyone will want to read this story. I hope that someone will want to read it, but more important, I have written it.

For almost twenty-two years, I have had this information in my head. I have written some poetry and a short piece or two about the events, but I did not find a way to tell the complete story until now. I was previously a teacher consultant for the Southern Nevada Writing Project and facilitated a university class to help teachers become better teachers of writing. I remember when I first joined the group and heard someone say, "Often, the stories we write are not the ones we have chosen but the ones that have chosen us." I know this statement to be true. This story would not let me alone until I wrote it.

Though I have written it in both third- and first-person narratives, many voices have told the story. It is told as realistic fiction and memoir because I don't know all the details—probably never will. Most of the players are gone now. Two of my brothers, Richard's sons, still do not know that I exist, but they will someday.

This story has occupied my thoughts and emotions for all these years, and getting it out on paper has liberated me from the sometimes-painful captivity that I have endured under its weight. Within its layers in my mind, it has held tinges of fear, doubt, and wonder. It has fought battles with my emotions over my inability to remain true to the story. I worried about offending someone or estranging someone because I have wanted and needed to reveal the truth. Whether every last detail of the story is true is no longer an issue for me. You see, this is my truth. This is what I've forged in my mind for what seems an interminable amount of time. This is how I have come to terms with who I am and how I came to be. This is how I have come to live with it all.

PART I

Disillusionment and Despair

Lost and alone, feeling drained,
Crying out in fear and pain.
Lord, are you there?
Does anyone care?
How do I go on,
Living trapped in despair?

CHAPTER 1

The Morning After

Kathleen leaned heavily against the doorframe, breathing in the early morning mist from the fog that had still not cleared. She was desperately trying to capture enough of the ocean air to buoy her up and help her get through the day. The boys were still asleep, and that was a blessing. She lit the cigarette that had grown moist from her hand and ventured out to the porch steps to smoke and to think.

After the first deep drag, she threw her head back, closed her eyes, and blew out the remnants of her placebo for peace. As she did so, images of the previous evening played before her eyes. How could she have let herself get into this situation again? He had looked so good and was so kind. Surely, he had feelings for her. But when he had dropped her off, just three hours earlier, he had made no mention of another date. Was this just another fling? Why did it feel like the morning after?

"Mom, Mom," the boys gleefully called as they wiped the sleepers from their eyes and raced out to the porch, where their mother sat slumped, wiping tears from her bloodshot orbs. They were such good boys, such sweet boys. Though life was difficult for this single mother, her boys did not cause this difficulty. Of course, she did have to feed and clothe them, but the love they gave back to her was all that kept her going, kept her alive. They snuggled into her on the steps and waited for her greeting.

"How are you this fine September morning, Michael and Steven? Did you like the babysitter last night? How late did she let you stay up?"

The five- and six-year-olds giggled as they remembered their fun evening, and Michael, the elder of the two, answered, "It wasn't very late, Mom."

Steven was starving and couldn't wait any longer to let it be known. "Mom, can I have some cereal?" he trumpeted. Kathleen's mind, clouded from guilt, worry, and lack of sleep, slowly comprehended as she arose from the step to make her way to the kitchen. Once inside the door, she realized that she had forgotten to get milk.

"Michael, we're out of milk. Go over to Mrs. Turner's house and ask if we can borrow some. Take the plastic measuring cup with you, and ask her to fill it up."

"Okay, Mom," he replied as he scampered across the gravel pathway that separated the two houses.

Kathleen walked into the kitchen to pour the cereal and to get the apple juice from the refrigerator. Her eyes fell on the blushing bowl of peaches set on the shelf before her. Richard had brought them to her. His family owned an orchard on the edge of town, and he had given her some freshly picked. "Peaches instead of flowers, hmm," she muttered as she grabbed one from the bowl and dug her teeth into the sweet, juicy flesh of the fruit. "Well, at least we can eat these," she concluded as she turned back to the counter to pour the juice for the boys.

Michael was carefully making his way back across the path, trying hard not to spill a drop of milk. Kathleen met him at the door, just in time to hear Mrs. Turner's nagging reminder, "Michael, tell your mother that she owes me two quarts now!" Kathleen rolled her eyes as she met her son with a smile.

"Thanks, honey. We'll get Mrs. Turner her milk when we go to the store this afternoon. Okay?" Michael smiled and ducked under his mom's arm to join his brother at the table. Kathleen poured the milk over the corn flakes and joined the boys at the table, where she finished her peach and sat watching their gleeful innocence. A smile gradually replaced her look of nervous preoccupation as she announced to her princes, "It's Sunday, boys, and we're going to go over to Lovers Point for a wienie roast. How does that sound?" She laughed, for she already knew what their answer would be.

"Yippee!" they yelled as they slurped up the last of the cereal and ran to their bedroom to put on play clothes.

A day at the beach will do us all some good, Kathleen thought as she carried the dishes to the sink, but then almost as suddenly as getting shot through the heart, other thoughts flooded her mind. *What if I'm pregnant? Mom and Dad will kill me. What will I do?*

CHAPTER 2

Reflection at Water's Edge

The fog lifted a little after noon, and the bright summer sun started to warm the white sandy beach. Kathleen lay on her stomach directly on the sand, her chin resting on her folded arms in front of her, as she consciously dug her toes down until she could feel the wet coolness. It was a glorious Monterey day in 1955. Sea otters cavorted in the distance, and the occasional roar of a sea lion could be heard above the screeches of the gulls. Michael and Steven occupied themselves at the water's edge, running from the waves and digging for sand crabs. Up above at the park, Kathleen had claimed their picnic spot and had started the coals to cook the hot dogs. Nothing could spoil such a day.

Still sleepy from her date the night before, Kathleen began to doze. She fought the desire for sleepy forgetfulness, as she heard the boys laughing in the near distance. The smell of the coals brought back the memory of her recent date with Richard. They went to a barbecue at a mutual friend's house—a friend from high school. Before the barbeque, she had a thought: *Who would ever believe that she was seeing Richard Ross, the nerd from the class of 1944?*

Richard had changed over the past twelve years. He was still the serious student type turned businessman, but his looks had improved tremendously. His steel-blue eyes and curly reddish-blond hair nicely adorned his six-foot-one muscular frame. He had inherited his father's investment business, had built a nice home, and had never married—not a bad catch for a thirty-year-old woman with two boys. Not bad at all. But Richard really was a cheapskate. Kathleen had looked forward to a big, juicy T-bone steak at the barbecue; instead, Richard brought two measly lamb chops.

While the men sat around drinking beer and talking sports, the women had brought out the rest of the dinner, all the while tittering about who was the most available bachelor. It came out in the conversation that Richard definitely had the most going for him. He had his father's well-established business and more than a promise to take over the peach orchards and ranch on the edge of town when his father was ready to give them up. Yes, he was ready to settle down, and more than one of the ladies present wanted to be the one.

After the barbecue, Richard and Kathleen had taken a ride along the beach and had come to a secluded spot beyond the harbor. The fog had already started to roll in, and the moon was hazy, providing only a glimmer of light. Friendly conversation and gentle kisses turned to passion on the beach, and Kathleen had given of herself freely. Richard had received her loving embraces without hesitation.

Richard was a childhood friend; surely, he had her best interests at heart. He knew of her past and her struggle to raise her two boys alone. He had also been friends with her first husband and knew of his abandonment just seven days after Michael's birth. He had heard of her bouts of depression and mania that had led her to the arms of many men, resulting in her second son's birth. Richard wouldn't take advantage of her too—not Richard.

The boys ran up to their mom, kicking sand on her back, bringing her back from her reverie. "Are you going to cook the hot dogs now, Mom?" Steven eagerly asked.

"Yes, sir!" Kathleen saluted as she jumped up from her warm habitation on the beach. "Race you to the table!" she screamed as she quickly ran up the hill to the grassy area above.

After their lunch of roasted wienies and pork and beans, the boys went back to the beach for shell hunting, and Kathleen went back to her spot and to her thoughts. *You would think I would learn,* she scolded herself. *Why do I always think that because they're nice to me, they're in love with me? What would Richard want with me and my two boys? He can have anybody he wants. There are plenty of single girls out there with no baggage. There were five of them at the barbecue last night alone. Damn, I am such a fool—a stupid little fool.* Though she knew that her negative thoughts did her no good, she couldn't keep herself from them. That was her pattern. A few days of mania made her commit such foolish acts, and then the depression would set in. She would spend interminable days berating herself for her self-inflicted pain and mistakes—each time lowering her self-esteem a little more—but then the mania would set in, and she'd go back for more. The cycle had become far too predictable, and although she hated herself for it, she felt powerless to stop it. Maybe it would stop now.

Maybe Richard would stay in her life, and things would get better. Yes, Richard would make all the bad memories go away. With a new daddy in her life, all would be well.

CHAPTER 3

Back to Reality

Monday morning came much too early. The alarm sounded, startling Kathleen to wakefulness and a sudden urge to vomit. As she ran to the bathroom, she wondered how she was going to get the boys to school and go on to work.

After losing the contents of her already-empty stomach, she went back to the bed to lie down on her pillow. *What did I eat last night? Oh, I didn't eat last night. The last thing I ate was the hot dog and beans at the beach. No wonder I feel sick.* After a few minutes, she maneuvered herself back to the bathroom to draw a bath and then proceeded to the boys' room to wake them up. Michael and Steven were always eager to go to school and jumped up before their mother had the chance to call them again. Michael pulled on his jeans and sweatshirt while Steven went to the kitchen to have his morning cereal. Meanwhile, Kathleen bathed, dressed, and went to the kitchen to pack the boys' lunches before she would walk them to school and then catch the bus to work.

Kathleen worked as a secretary for an architectural firm and was quite good at her job. English and business had been her best subjects in high school, and it showed in her daily performance and yearly reviews. Because she had no other source of income, it was important that she keep this job. Though her budget was always tight, she somehow managed to have a few pennies left over at the end of each month.

The bus ride over to the business district seemed especially long this morning as her earlier nausea attempted to return. Arriving at her stop, she quickly exited the bus, and upon entering the office, she ran right past Sally, the other secretary in the office, without even a "good morning." After a couple of minutes, Sally knocked on the restroom door to see if Kathleen was all right. Upon the second knock, her question was answered as she heard Kathleen's heaving on the other side of the door. Sally walked back to her desk and waited for Kathleen to come out of the restroom.

"Are you all right?" Sally inquired in a concerned voice as Kathleen entered the office with tear-streaked eyes and broken blood vessels in her cheeks. Collapsing into her chair, Kathleen clearly was anything but all right.

"I ate a hot dog at the beach yesterday, and I think that made me sick to my stomach. I woke up feeling ill; I thought it was going away, but it came back on the bus."

"Maybe you should take the day off, Kathleen. You don't look so good."

"I really can't do that, Sally. You know that Mr. Gibson is counting on me to finish up the Taylor account this morning, and besides, rent is due Friday. I need the money."

"Well, I could cover for you. It's not like I haven't finished off an account before."

"I'm going to try to stay, at least until lunchtime, Sally. Thanks for the offer. If it gets too bad, I may just take you up on it."

"Okay, Kathleen, but don't push yourself."

Kathleen grabbed a peppermint from the candy jar on Mr. Gibson's desk and started her day's work. Soon, she got so busy that she didn't have time to think about how she was feeling. She closed the Taylor account by noon and retired to the lunchroom to eat her sandwich. Surprisingly, the peanut butter and jelly tasted good to her, and when she was through eating, the nausea had completely disappeared.

At about 1:00 p.m., Mr. Gibson walked in and announced, "Ladies, we did quite well on the Taylor job, and because of our success, I'm giving you the afternoon off! Go shopping, treat yourselves to a matinee, whatever makes you happy." Sally and Kathleen stared at each other in amazement and grabbed their purses before their boss had time to change his mind. "See you in the morning, girls," he called after them, "9:00 a.m. sharp!" They looked at each other and giggled as they left the office and went their separate ways.

Kathleen took advantage of her two hours of free time before she had to go get the boys from school. A nap was just the thing. Though she was feeling better than she had earlier, she was now extremely tired. Yes, a nap would surely solve the problem.

Kicking off her shoes as she entered the house, Kathleen quickly undressed and lay down on the cool sheets. A musty odor in the room required her to get back up to open the window for some fresh air. Once she lay back on the bed, she began to wonder about Richard. *How does he feel about our date? Will he call me again?* Then, in an effort to mask any future disappointment, she stated aloud, "Oh, what do I care? It was a night out, even if we only had lamb chops. He wasn't bad, but I've had better." At that point, she put him out of her mind and drifted off to sleep.

Kathleen was awakened by the telephone ringing. "Hello," she uttered drowsily.

"Kathleen, it's Mom. What are you doing home this time of the day?" Ada inquired.

"Oh, Mom, hi. I got off early because we finished a big job today. I was just taking a nap before I go get the boys. Why did you call me at home if you thought I wouldn't be here?"

"Well, I already tried you at work, and your boss said you had left. I couldn't imagine why unless something was wrong with Michael or Steven."

"No, Mom, they're fine. In fact, I need to leave in a few minutes to go get them. What did you call about?"

"Well, you said that you'd call to let me know how your date went with Mr. Bigshot Ross. How did it go?"

"It was nothing too special, Mom. He brought lamb chops to the barbecue while everyone else was eating steak. I could barely choke them down. His crowd is pretty snobby, not people I'd want to spend too much time with."

"What did you do after the party?"

"We went for a drive, and then he took me home."

"So, you had an early night?"

"Not really early. We talked for a while, you know, about the old days, and caught up on what's happened since high school."

"Do you like him?"

"I don't know, Mom. He's been a bachelor too long. I'm not sure what I think of him."

"Are you going to see him again?"

"Yeah, sure, Mom. I probably will."

"Did he make another date with you?" she seemed to interrogate.

"Not yet, but it's only been two days. I'm sure he'll call again."

"So, what time did you say you got home?"

"I didn't say, Mom, but I think it was a little past midnight."

"Did he kiss you good night?"

"Mom, why all the questions? I think that's about all that I have time to answer. I need to go get the boys now."

"Kathleen?"

"Yes, Mom?"

"Did you . . . ?"

"Mom. I have to go now. Good-bye."

CHAPTER 4

Nothing Else from You

Two weeks later, she still hadn't heard from Richard. It had been five years since she had given birth to Steven, and Kathleen could no longer ignore the early signs of pregnancy. The missed period was the biggest clue besides the nausea, exhaustion, frequent urination, and tender breasts. She couldn't confirm for sure for a couple of weeks still, but she really didn't need a test to know. She knew, and it wasn't good news.

For one thing, her mother and father would probably disown her. They had practically done so when Steven came along. It had taken three years for them to forgive her for not going away and giving him up for adoption. Then, there was the issue of money. She couldn't afford to go to the doctor. She barely made enough to take care of herself and the two boys she already had. Though she didn't want to think about it, there was another reason why this news disturbed her. The family's reputation was at stake. The gossip had just recently died down about Steven's illegitimate birth. If this was happening, she'd have to leave town. She couldn't put her family nor her boys through the embarrassment, not again.

Before she made any decisions, she needed to talk to Richard. Maybe if he knew the situation, his feelings would change. He came from a good family; they would want him to do the right thing. She knew that he cared about her. You didn't make love to someone like he did if you didn't care. Maybe he had just been busy. Yes, that was it. He had been busy with the business and hadn't had time to call. "I bet he'd be thrilled if I called him," she assured herself as she nibbled on a saltine from the box that she now kept on the bedside table.

The next afternoon afforded her just the time she needed to make that call. Mr. Gibson had gone out on an inspection, and Sally had gone to the building department to pull some permits. Kathleen called Information for Richard's work number and took a deep breath before she dialed. After the fourth ring, she was about to hang up when a familiar voice answered, "Hello. Ross Investments."

Nervously, she replied, "Richard, is that you?"

"Uh-huh, yes. Kathleen, how are you?"

"I was surprised to hear you answer. Aren't secretaries supposed to do that?" she teased.

"Oh yeah, well, Anne took a late lunch today, so I'm manning all stations right now."

"Oh, I see. Well, I hadn't heard from you, and I was wondering how you are."

"I'm doing well, Kathleen, and yourself?"

"Not too badly, Richard."

"And the boys?"

"They're great, as always."

"Good, good, I'm glad to hear it. So, to what do I owe this pleasure?"

"Well, Richard, I hope it really is a pleasure. I just wanted you to know what a lovely time I had on our date a couple of weeks ago. I thought I would hear from you before now, but I figured you had been busy with business. Just wanted to see how you are."

"I'm fine, Kathleen, and yes, I have been very busy—extremely busy."

"I was wondering if I might reciprocate and ask you out on a date."

"Really? Huh. Well, let me check my schedule. When were you thinking about our getting together?"

"This Friday works for me. How about you?"

"Hmm, this Friday? No, I have something else planned, you know, with the family, this Friday."

"How about Saturday?"

"Saturday? Let me see. Man, Kathleen, that day is booked up as well."

"Sunday? Would Sunday work? I could prepare a picnic for the beach."

"Kathleen, no, Sunday will not work."

"You have something planned for Sunday as well?"

"No, I don't have anything planned, but I can't see you."

Kathleen gulped down the feeling of despair that was beginning to rise higher in her throat as she asked, "You can't see me? Why not, Richard?"

"Well, you see . . . You know my secretary, Anne? You know—she was at the party the other night. Well, you see, we have been seeing each other, and I finally got up the nerve to ask her to be my steady. We have been seeing each other on and off for a couple of years, and it has taken me this long to figure out what I wanted to do about it."

At this declaration, Kathleen sat frozen, motionless at her desk. Her mind filled with confusion that was quickly turning to rage.

"Kathleen, you still there? Kathleen, did you hear what I said?"

"Oh, yes, Richard, I heard every word—perfectly fine, perfectly clear! What I want to know is why you slept with me if you already had these feelings for her?"

Now, Richard was the one having a hard time summoning the words. Sheepishly, he answered, "Well, you know, Kathleen. We had a little too much to drink. It was a nice night, and I don't know—it just happened."

"It just *happened*? I've known you since we were kids! We hadn't seen each other for twelve years! I thought you had feelings for me! You think that I'm that easy—that I just sleep with anyone?" she screamed into the phone.

"Hey, Kathleen, whoa, whoa—wait a minute. I asked you out on a date. When I saw you that day at the bank, I thought it would be fun to bring you to the party with some of our old friends. It was a reunion of sorts. I never said anything about a relationship. We aren't kids anymore. We're both adults. I thought that was understood."

"Oh, it's understood now, Richard. I'm sorry I bothered you! I just thought that you might like to know that I'm expecting your baby!"

Silence. Richard was speechless, and then, suddenly, he became defensive. "You're what? It's only been two weeks. How could you know this so soon?"

"You forget, Richard, that I have been through this two times before. I am pregnant."

"Kathleen, I don't know how to say this without just saying it—are you sure it's mine?"

This was a blow that Kathleen did not expect, and she couldn't just let it go. "What the hell are you suggesting, Richard? Do you think that there's a chance that I have been with someone else recently? What do you think I am, some cheap whore? Is that what you think, you bastard? No! You aren't going to get off that easy! It's your baby, all right. It's yours whether you believe it or not, and maybe you need to tell Anne about it!"

"Now, wait a minute, Kathleen. Calm down. Let's talk about this.

Okay, maybe it is my baby. What do you want me to do? Do you want some money? How much do you need, Kathleen?" he asked while wiping perspiration from his brow.

"I don't want your money, Richard! I don't want anything else from you," she sobbed into the phone. "I thought you'd do the right thing when you found out. I thought you'd want to be a father to your child! I was crazy! How could I have thought that you were any different from the rest? I—I have nothing more to say to you! Good-bye, Richard."

"Uh—good-bye, Kathleen. If you need, uh, some money, let me know," he assured her as he shook his head while returning the receiver to its cradle.

Feeling broken and extremely disturbed and defenseless, Kathleen slammed down the phone and tore out of the office.

The next few days were a blur. Kathleen did not show up for work, and the boys did not attend school. They ate cereal and watched TV, and she slept unceasingly. When the nosy neighbor noticed that their usual routine had been broken, she called the police, and an officer came to the house. Who should that officer be but Kathleen's own brother, Trent Terrell?

Michael answered the door to see his uncle Trent standing there in his police uniform. "Hi, Uncle Trent. What are you doing here?"

"I was just stopping by to check on you guys, Mike. Where's your mom?"

"Oh, she's asleep. She isn't feeling very well."

"How long has she been sleeping, Mike?"

"I don't know—maybe a couple of days, Uncle Trent."

"Okay, you go back to the television. I'm going to check on your mom."

"Okay, Uncle Trent."

Trent entered his sister's bedroom, not knowing what to expect. He found her lying perfectly still on the bed, and upon closer inspection, he could see that her eyes were sunken and that her breathing was faint. Immediately, he got on the radio and called for an ambulance. Within minutes, Kathleen was on her way to the hospital, and the boys were picked up by their grandmother.

CHAPTER 5

Weeping for Childish Ignorance

Kathleen was spared the pain of telling her family the news. When she awoke a few days later, she found the family knew of her condition and had rallied to support her. Ada and Tom, her father, and Trent were all there when she groggily opened her eyes. She immediately closed them again as she began to recognize her surroundings. She knew that she was in the hospital and that something was terribly wrong. Instinctively, she reached for her abdomen.

Ada spoke first. "Kathleen, you're going to be okay, and so is the baby."

Why is everyone being so nice? she thought. *They weren't nice last time,* she silently reflected.

Her father spoke next. "Honey, you need to get your strength back. Mom and I will watch the boys until you feel better. When you get out, we'll talk about what to do."

What to do? What did her father mean by that? Of course, she was going to have a baby. She didn't have much choice about that. As she blankly gazed at the group, they all stood, and they began to say good-bye and file out of the room—all but her brother Trent.

"Kathleen, when you are feeling better, we'll talk about this. You knew you were pregnant, right? Who is the father, Sis? Do you know? Mom thought it might be Richard Ross. Is that who it is?"

Kathleen heard her brother's questions, but she did not acknowledge them. After a few minutes, he squeezed her hand, kissed her on the forehead, and rose to go. "I'll come by tomorrow, Sis. I love you." A single tear escaped her left eye and rolled down her cheek.

Alone in her darkened hospital room, Kathleen wept bitter tears of despair and self-pity. The depression was beginning to loosen its hold on her now that she was once again hydrated, well fed, and rested. No longer numb or deadened to all feeling, she felt all the conflicting feelings that had rendered her helpless in the past weeks rise within her. She wept for her fostered children, the loves of her life; she wept for her childish ignorance and her inability to learn from past mistakes; and she wept for the life that grew within her that nobody wanted. Remembering her brother's parting words, she wept even more profusely. "I love you," he had said. She couldn't remember the last time she had heard those words.

The weeping worked its catharsis on Kathleen's troubled soul, and feeling temporarily relieved of all her burdens and responsibilities, she fell into a deep sleep, the best sleep that she had gotten in weeks. Her body lay completely relaxed across the bed, unlike previous nights spent knotted in the fetal position. Her regular breathing and strong pulse had returned the healthy glow to her pallid cheeks, and peaceful dreams danced across her subconscious, though she would not remember them upon waking. This night, Kathleen felt free of worry and concern. Tomorrow, she would have many answers to give and decisions to make, but this night was hers alone, a time of renewal and hope of relief.

CHAPTER 6

Something You Can Do for Me

Morning crept into Kathleen's window early and awakened the activity of the hospital's daily routines. After a hearty breakfast of scrambled eggs, ham, oatmeal, orange segments, and hot tea, and her first shower in days, Kathleen almost felt like herself again. She sat on the bed, brushing her thick brown hair, which was warmed by the sunlight coming in her window. Her thoughts went to her boys and the hope that she would see them soon.

As she imagined their joyful reunion, a tall, slender man in his late twenties, dressed in a white coat and reviewing a patient's chart, walked over to the side of her bed near the window. Looking into her questioning eyes, he cheerfully inquired, "How are you feeling today, Kathleen? The nurses say that you had a peaceful night's rest."

"I am feeling better today, Dr. —." She searched for his name tag or badge.

"Oh, it's Dr. Samuels. I'm sorry; I guess that we haven't officially met, though I've been fairly close by since you arrived a couple of days ago. You were having a pretty rough time."

"Well, Dr. Samuels, I'm ready to go home. When can you let me out of here?"

"I would be happy to let you go home but not before we have a plan to handle your disorder. I have a few questions to ask you. We have some things to discuss so that we can proceed."

"Proceed? Proceed with what, Doctor? I'm pregnant, and I'm going to have a baby. That's already been decided."

"Yes, you are carrying what seems to be a healthy fetus, but I'm not so sure that this pregnancy is healthy for you or the baby. These bouts of depression cannot continue if you hope to remain healthy and take care of the children that you already have."

"I don't understand, Dr. Samuels. What is it that you are trying to say?"

"Kathleen, before I say anything more, I need to ask you some questions about yourself. I have gotten some information from your family, but I need to hear about it from your perspective. Some of what I will ask you may be painful, but if I am to help you, I need to have the answers."

"What do you want to know, Doctor? I'll do the best I can."

"Well, Kathleen, I suspect that you are suffering from a condition known as *manic depression* (now known as *bipolar disorder*). Many things can bring it on, and we believe that in some cases, it is even hereditary. It is a type of psychosis that involves severe mood swings, so severe that at times, you might do things that seem completely out of character. That is the manic phase of the illness. I'm sure that I don't have to tell you about the depression side of it. You have been experiencing an extremely severe bout with it for about a week now. When I described these symptoms to your family, they seemed to agree with my diagnosis. It seems that you have been suffering with this for about six or seven years, ever since your husband left you and your newborn son."

Kathleen stared at this man of medicine, wondering where he had come from and how he knew her so well. For as long as she could remember, she hadn't understood the way she was. She didn't remember when it started. But as she reached way back in her memories to the time that Raymond had left her, it began to make sense. She had experienced a couple of breakdowns and gone home to her parents' house for several months. She had been unable to care for the baby or for herself. She had been entirely helpless. After a couple of months, things seemed to get better; she began to work and moved into her own apartment with the baby, but that's when she started with the men. One after another, they visited her bed and trampled on her heart, and one left her with Steven. She had never been sure which one was the father. Now, it had happened again.

"Dr. Samuels, is there something that you can do for me?"

"Kathleen, I believe that there is a great deal that I can do for you. The first thing that I'd like to do is put you on some medication that will lessen the severity of the mood swings. I also strongly suggest that you come weekly for counseling so that you can learn how to better deal with this. Something that has me a bit concerned is the pregnancy. The drugs that I want to try are relatively new. Not much is known about their effect on a developing fetus. This might sound a bit insensitive, though I assure you that it is not meant to be: Do you want to have this baby?"

The doctor's question surprised Kathleen. She had never considered not having the baby, although she had not really considered having it either. With her bouts of nausea and her conversation with Richard, and of course her family's probable reaction to the news, she had not really thought beyond the moment. She had been too busy reacting to the pregnancy to think about it.

"Dr. Samuels, I was raised with a strict Catholic upbringing. I'm sure that I don't have to tell you what that means. Not having this baby is not an option. I've made some mistakes, but I don't think they qualify me for eternal damnation."

"Kathleen, I was just suggesting that your medical condition may indicate a strong reason to discontinue the pregnancy. I am not telling you that that's what you should do. That decision is between you and God. I'm only here to help you with whatever you decide. However, I do need to tell you that you only have a few weeks to make that decision. After that, it will be too late."

"I certainly didn't plan on being in this situation again. God knows my family is disappointed and unhappy with me, but I am pregnant. And as you have said, Doctor, the decision of what to do is between me and God. I will have this baby. I don't know what I'll do afterward, but the baby will be born."

"Okay, Kathleen, that is your choice, but you must understand that this will not be as easily treated without medication. Until at least the second trimester, I do not recommend you taking anything. It could greatly affect the developing fetus. After that, we'll see. For now, we will try to control the mood swings with diet and exercise, and I do want you to come in for counseling once a week."

"Doctor, I don't know how I can pay for that. I barely make it each month as it is, and I've been out of work for almost a week now."

"Well, you are in luck, Kathleen. I am doing a study with the university on manic depression, and if you'll agree to be part of that study, your sessions will be free of charge. What do you say to that?"

Feeling supported by her doctor's care and concern, Kathleen admitted, "I say that things are looking up, Doc. Thank you for all that you've done. I just might make it through this after all."

CHAPTER 7

A Change of Plans

With a counseling session behind her and feeling more positive about her future, Kathleen called her brother to see if he could pick her up from the hospital. Trent was almost done with his shift and would arrive soon. Before going home, she needed to get a few groceries and pick up the boys from their grandparents' home. Trent arrived within an hour, and they went on their way. Milk, bread, cereal, hamburger, macaroni, a few vegetables, and some apple juice would do them for now. It felt so good to be out of the hospital that even a trip to the market felt like an outing to Kathleen.

As they pulled up in front of her parents' home, she noticed that her oldest brother's car was there. Wondering why Lee would be off work so early, Kathleen and Trent walked up to the front door. When they reached it, the door opened, and Michael and Steven ran to their mother, wrapping their arms around her middle and not letting go. This welcome brought a few tears to Kathleen's eyes, and once they got in the door, she knelt in front of them to talk at their level.

"I'm sorry that I've been gone so long, boys, but the doctor has me feeling better now. I'm anxious for us to go back home. Are you ready?" Michael and Steven's eager little heads nodded, and they ran to the bedroom where they had been staying to gather their belongings that their grandmother had already packed.

Lee stood up and moved over closer to Kathleen now seated on the couch. "Kathleen, Mom tells me that you've been having another bout and that you're pregnant again. Is that true?"

"Yes, Lee, it is true. My doctor wants to put me in a study for my disorder, and it won't cost any money. He says that there is a lot more hope than there used to be for people with manic depression."

"Mom also said that the doctor suggested that you not have the baby in order to be treated," Lee stated.

"He actually said that I can't take the medicine that he wants me on until after the second trimester, which will be in about five months," Kathleen corrected.

"And what are you going to do in the meantime since you've decided to have the baby? What are *we* going to do in the meantime?" Lee snarled.

Kathleen looked around the room and into the faces of her parents and her brothers, calming herself before she very carefully phrased her answer. "I'm not sure what you mean exactly, Lee. I plan to go back to my house tonight, talk to my boss about where I've been, and hope that I still have a job."

"Are you going to stay in town, then, and keep this baby too?" Lee belabored his point.

"I don't know about the baby yet, but I will have it and start treatment with my doctor as soon as it's safe," Kathleen returned with her head held high.

"Let me make this clear, Kathleen. This is not the first time that this has happened—I'm sure you know! We live in a pretty small town where everyone knows everyone else's business, whether that's right or not. Last time this happened, it caused quite a stir in the town, at our jobs, just trying to go out in public. Even though it has been five years, I think that it has been just over a year now since someone at work asked me to set him up with my runaround sister," Lee said, seething.

At this point, Kathleen had heard enough and stood up, calling the boys to come; they were leaving. Trent stood up as well and took the boys' bags and started for the front door. Kathleen uttered a good-bye to her mom and dad and let Lee know how she felt about his subtle reminders. "I'm sorry that you have had to endure so much because of me, Lee, but I haven't done any of this to bring shame on you!"

Once they got into the car, Kathleen was shaking, and Trent grabbed her hand closest to him. "I'm sorry, Sis, that Lee said all of that to you. You didn't need to hear it again, in my opinion, but Mom got him all stirred up by suggesting that he put you in some home until after you've had the baby."

Kathleen looked up with tears streaming down her face and questioned, "You mean that they want to have me committed? They want me out of the way to save face—to leave my boys with them—so they can act as though nothing is going on?" her incredulity coming out more strongly with each uttered word.

As she stated what they had in mind for her, Trent could only motion affirmatively. By now, the boys were curled up in the back seat, sleeping soundly as though absolutely nothing threatened their world.

Pulling up in front of her place, Kathleen could see a note on the front door. "Oh, damn! I'm pretty sure that's an eviction notice! Rent was due last Friday, but I was in the hospital and haven't even picked up my check to pay it!" Shaking her head in disbelief, Kathleen blurted, "You know, Trent, I need to get out of here. I don't trust Lee, and it's clear that they don't want me here anyway. Where can I go? Up north? Do you know anyone in the city that I could stay with for a few days until I find a place and figure out what to do?"

With just a couple of seconds to consider her question, Trent answered, "Sis, I actually do. A friend of mine on the force has a sister who lives in San Francisco and is looking for a roommate. You might all have to stay in the same room, but at least you can start out there for a week or two. Let me call him and see about taking you up there tonight. I know that you don't have any of your things, but I should be able to get into your house tomorrow and go by your work to pick up your last check. I could drive back up tomorrow night with it all. What do you think?" Trent waited cautiously for his sister's response.

Looking again at her front door and then back at her hands in her lap, she reached up to wipe the falling tears and whispered, "Trent, I don't know how I got so lucky as to have you for my brother. I'm sure that I've embarrassed you too, but you just keep on loving me and trying to help me in any way that you can." Remembering Lee's threatening looks and words, she quickly agreed, "Yes, I think we should do as you've suggested. Let's go."

PART II

Hope and Fulfillment

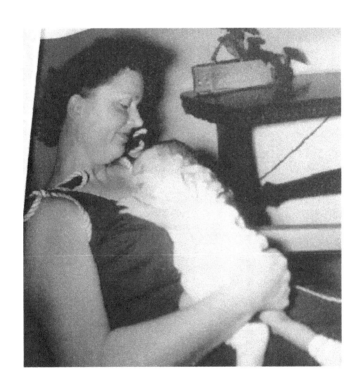

Little one, so small and new,
All my life, I've dreamed of you.
Your downy skin and curly hair,
How did I manage without you there?

CHAPTER 8

No Ordinary Man

Charles Howell was an average man by the world's standards. He had been on his own since age twelve, never finished high school, eloped at seventeen, and worked physically laborious jobs all his life. If he truly felt that he had never accomplished anything great, he would have been the first to say so. But Charles didn't feel that way. He didn't feel that way at all. By his standards, he was the richest a man could be. He had been married to the same loving and devoted wife for fifty-one years, was the proud father of a daughter who had met all his expectations and more, and was "Papa" to four delightful grandchildren. No, Charles didn't listen to the world, and he wasn't interested in its judgment of him. He always did what he thought best, and that included the day in 1955 when he had decided to invest in his future—in a baby girl he could call his own.

Charles and Thelma, his beautiful wife, were born and raised in Oklahoma, right in the middle of the Great Depression. Charles was the eldest of three children, and Thelma was sandwiched in between two brothers. His father leased oil wells, and her dad was a rancher who drove cattle to market. The day he first saw her in the small office of the telephone company, he knew she had to be his. She agreed, and in the first month of 1938, they became husband and wife.

With the anticipation of the United States entering WWII, the draft was in full swing. Charles preferred to enlist in his chosen branch of the armed services, the Navy Seabees, and he was off to basic training. His first assigned base was in Rhode Island, where they rented a room from an Italian family and where Thelma went to work for the war effort in assembling plane instrument panels. One day while out on maneuvers in the frigid Atlantic, Charles's boat overturned, and he and his squad spent a long night treading water until they were rescued the next day. The cold water had caused nerve damage to Charles's back, and before long, he was honorably discharged and back to civilian life.

For a while, they remained close to their families, living in the same town and helping to raise their younger siblings during economically tough times, but when Pappy Howell decided to move to California to drill water and oil wells there, Charles and Thelma had to take him up on the offer of a job and a new adventure. By then, his younger sister and her older brother had married, and nieces and nephews were on the way. However, Charles and Thelma, even after several years of marriage, had not conceived a child. They loved the nieces and nephews as their own and often helped out by taking the kids for long weekends to give their parents a break, but when the weekend ended, it was just the two of them again, with their empty nest bubbling over with love that they needed to share.

Once they had celebrated five years of marriage, they decided to try to find out why they still had no baby on the way. In preliminary questioning and testing, it was discovered that when Charles had come down with the mumps in his early teenage years, without proper care during the illness, it had rendered him sterile. The news greatly disappointed this couple, who had so much love to give a child, and they began to address the possibility of adoption.

A few months after their move to California, Charles and Thelma decided to apply for adoption with the state. One of the requirements for adoption was the ability to show stability. Charles and Thelma moved around quite a bit as they followed the drilling jobs and attributed that as the cause for their not being called in for an adoption interview.

The drilling business started out well, but after a decade, they didn't have enough income to support them, his parents, and his sister's family. When Charles learned of mining opportunities in Arizona, he and Thelma decided to try their luck in the little railroad town of Kingman. In 1954, for the second time in their lives, they were completely on their own in a small desert town in the middle of nowhere, but sixteen years of marriage had cemented an already-strong relationship, preparing them for the challenges they would meet.

CHAPTER 9

The Watchman

Charles quitclaimed an area known for gold, silver, and uranium deposits in Mohave County. He named it the Green Weenie mine. Due to its inaccessibility by road, he had to hire a pilot to fly him into the area. Stan Harris, a local pilot, had a small prop plane and accompanied Charles on several trips to the mine. During one such flight, the subject of children came up. Stan and his wife had been unable to conceive and had hired an attorney to search for a baby in California. The process that Stan explained intrigued Charles, and he wondered about the prospect of acquiring a child for him and Thelma the same way. Their discussion turned serious, and Stan became the watchman for a child for Charles and Thelma as well.

On a December evening in 1955, Charles received a call from Stan. They were to fly to the mine in a few days, so he thought the call concerned their upcoming trip; however, the call brought news of another nature.

"Chuck?" Stan enthusiastically addressed.

"Yes, Stan. How are you? Do we have a problem with the trip?"

"No, Chuck, no problem at all. You remember our discussion last time we went to the mine, about adoption?"

"Sure do, Stan. How could I forget that?"

"Well, I told you I'd keep an eye out for you, and you won't believe what happened!"

"What's that, Stan? Did you get a baby?"

"No, Chuck, I have two babies! One is due in four months and the other in six. My wife and I have decided to take the one that is due in four, and I was wondering if you'd like to see about the one due in June."

"Uh—well, I am quite surprised. I can't talk right now because Thelma is in the next room, but I am interested. Can we talk on Saturday when we fly to the mine? Do you know anything about the circumstances?"

"All I know is that the mother is twenty-nine, unmarried, and from a good family in California. She has two other children and is unable to care for another."

Learning of this mother in desperate need and quickly calculating his current obligations, Charles assured him, "Stan, I am definitely interested. Please put this on hold until Saturday. I will be able to give you my answer then."

"Okay, Chuck. Until Saturday, buddy. Good-bye."

Charles was overcome with emotion at the possibility. After seventeen years of marriage and at thirty-five years of age, the opportunity to finally have a baby of their own had seemed like too much to hope for. He wanted to shout the news to Thelma, but nothing was definite yet. He was very protective of his wife, and he didn't want her to suffer the disappointment if things didn't work out. Oh, but from the moment they hung up the phone that night, dreams and plans flew through his head both day and night! He'd whisper to himself, "A baby. Could it really be?"

By Saturday, the anticipation was almost too much to bear. Stan had found out a bit more information about the birth mother and had the number of the attorney who would handle the adoption. The mother was of French descent and came from a large Catholic family in the Bay Area. She had had to quit her job, and she had no money coming in. She was asking for money for her rent, food, doctor bills, and the delivery. Charles knew that this wouldn't come cheap, but he knew that he could handle it.

"So, what do you think, Chuck? Are you going to go through with it?" Stan asked him.

"I don't see how I can pass up the chance, Stan. We've waited so long. I think that we had given up hope that we could ever be parents, though we don't talk about it much anymore."

"You think you'd better tell Thelma about it first—I mean, before you call the attorney?"

"I probably should, Stan, but I don't think I will. Let's see how it goes first. I'm going to give it a couple of months to make sure the mother doesn't change her mind and the pregnancy continues to go well. Then I'll tell her."

"Okay, Chuck. Here's the number of the attorney. He'll take care of the arrangements and communicate with the birth mother for you."

Grasping the small square of paper in his hand like his life depended on it, Charles uttered, "This is too good to be true, Stan. How can I ever thank you?"

"You don't have anything to thank me for, Chuck. You and Thelma are too good of people not to have a child of your own to love."

CHAPTER 10

Ultimate Surprise

How Charles concealed the news from his wife for four months was a miracle in itself. When they'd go downtown to shop on Saturdays, he couldn't help but scan the baby department out of the corner of his eye. A pair of little red cowboy boots was first on his list to buy. He saw the Navajo children prints, with their chubby little faces and gleaming smiles, and thought they'd look so cute in the nursery, whether they had a boy or a girl. Every time he thought about a baby coming soon, goose bumps would well up on his flesh, and he'd get the warmest feeling around his heart.

All went according to plan. The pregnancy was developing nicely, and Charles had even insisted on providing vitamins for the mother so that his little boy or girl would grow strong and healthy. He managed to make enough extra money at a second job as a diner short-order cook to make the monthly payments to the birth mother. According to the attorney, she was still on board, full steam ahead.

He knew he needed to tell Thelma that they had a baby on the way, but as the time neared, he became a bit unsure of how she would receive the news. He wondered if he had waited too long to tell her, but arranging this ultimate surprise for his sweetheart had become the best secret he had ever kept. Each day longer that he waited to tell her added to the excitement and anticipation of revealing his surprise.

Finally, some news came that let him know the time had come. One evening in late April, the telephone rang. It was Stan, and he was on his way to California. "Chuck?" he almost giggled.

"Hey, Stan. What's the good news?"

"Well, man, we just got the call. Our baby boy is here!"

Charles was almost as excited for himself as he was for Stan, for with the news came the realization that their own little bundle would be arriving in just eight weeks.

"Stan, I think I know how you must be feeling about now. I'm happy for you, man! Have a safe trip, and give me a call when you get back home with your little guy."

"Will do, Chuck. Bye."

As Charles ended the call and walked into the kitchen, Thelma was finishing up the dinner dishes and asked, "Who was that, honey? Your mother?"

Barely able to conceal his happiness, he answered, "No, dear, it wasn't Mom, but it was some very good news. It was my pilot, Stan. He and his wife are going to get their baby boy tonight!"

"Oh, honey, how wonderful for them! They must be on cloud nine!"

Rattling his car keys in his pocket, Charles answered, "Yes, I'm sure they are. Honey, are you about finished there? I'd like to go out for a drive tonight. We'll go get a root beer at A&W."

"That sounds great. Just give me a minute, dear."

Before Charles went out to start the car, he snuck to the hall closet to remove a package he had stored there some months before. Stowing the package under the driver's seat, he backed out the car, and they were on their way. It was a fragrant spring evening. The trees and flowers were blooming everywhere they looked, and a light wind disseminated their perfume for miles around. Arriving at the drive-in, they ordered their root beer floats and waited for the carhop to bring them back. "Floats, mmm," Thelma crooned. "It must be a special occasion!"

While they were waiting, Charles slid out the package from under his seat and placed it in Thelma's lap. "It is," he answered with a broad smile across his face.

"What's this?" she asked with a look of delight on her face.

"Open it up and see for yourself!" he instructed.

Charles watched Thelma's every movement as she slid her hand inside the paper bag and pulled out its contents. In her fingers, she held a tiny pair of red leather cowboy boots. She looked from the boots to Charles several times before she confusedly stated, "I don't understand. What are you telling me?"

The secret he had held so long could be held no longer. "Thelma," he gently announced, "we're going to have a baby."

He could see on her face that she couldn't believe what she had heard—that it couldn't be. Just as he couldn't stand the silence any longer, she thought out loud, "Did he say we are going to have a baby?"

Taking her hands in his own, he brought them to his lips and kissed them and answered, "Yes, honey, that's what I said. In late June, we are going to become parents!"

Charles imagined that Thelma couldn't begin to understand what he was telling her. "How could this be? What baby? Whose baby? When? Where?"

The questions came faster than he could answer them, and with each answer grew two distinct, conflicting emotions within her. The look on her face, though filled with wonderment, told Charles that she was finding something about the news hard to accept. As tears began to fall from her eyes, Charles asked, "Thelma, what's wrong? What are you thinking?"

He searched her face for her thoughts, as it took her a moment to collect herself before she answered him, slowly, deliberately, "Chuck, . . . I don't know if I can . . . love another woman's child."

They looked at each other for several minutes without saying a word. Her statement had taken him by surprise. Of all the reactions he had anticipated her having, this wasn't one of them. He sat there, dumbfounded, not knowing what to say. This was not something that he could talk her into. He had had time to think about this blessed event in their lives. She, on the other hand, had known nothing about it until this moment. It wasn't like getting a new puppy or a goldfish. This was a human life, a brand-new, helpless little life that would depend on them for everything for the rest of its life.

Charles had nothing more that he could say. He patted her hand, paid for the floats, and drove them home in silence. He knew that she needed time to think about all that he had sprung on her. Though happy news, it had been a shock to her, and she needed to get used to the idea. When they arrived home, they got ready for bed, kissed good night, and turned off the light, but one thing was certain: it would be quite some time before Thelma and Charles closed their eyes and fell asleep.

CHAPTER 11

A Time of Preparation

The next morning brought a noticeable change in Thelma's countenance. From the bedroom, he could hear her up and about, scurrying around the house as she did when she had much to accomplish. He arose and went to find her standing in the spare bedroom, looking around at all their possessions that they had stashed there. Seeing Charles, she inquired, "Did you say that this baby is coming in eight weeks? There is so much to do. We need to clear out this room, buy diapers, get a crib—oh, and the first thing we need to do is call our parents to tell them that they are going to be grandparents again!" Charles stood smiling at her marked enthusiasm. This was the Thelma he knew. This was the woman who loved children as much as he did. This was the woman who was to become the mother of his child. Their glee found its expression in laughter, and as they embraced, she reached up and whispered in his ear, "Thank you." These two simple words were all that he needed to hear to confirm in his heart that he had made the right decision.

As the weeks flew by, they filled each day with preparations for the arrival of their precious bundle: painting the room, buying the crib and the baby's layette, and choosing to decorate the room with the Navajo children theme. It really didn't take too long to get the baby's room ready for habitation because they focused all their energy on their special project for several weeks. Grandpa Howell would paint the bassinet as soon as they knew if it was a boy or a girl. They would drive to San Francisco when they got the call and drive back through Fresno for a stop at the paternal grandparents' home and first meeting with aunts, uncles, and cousins before heading back to Kingman.

With only a month left before the expected arrival, plans changed slightly when Thelma discovered a lump in her breast. She had not gone to the doctor for years, and because Kingman was such a small town with just one general practitioner, it was decided that she would go to Fresno to see a specialist there. The appointment was just two weeks before the baby was due. With bags packed, Charles watched Thelma as she stood in the doorway and took in every detail. They had all in place and ready for the baby to come home. Diapers and little clothes were washed and in the drawers; the crib was made and covered with a sheet to keep dust out; and the diaper bag was packed with all they needed to dress and prepare the baby for the trip home from the hospital, plus a few extra days' worth. They had attended to everything. At last, they were ready.

Charles grabbed Thelma's luggage to take her to the train station, but before they left, he had one more surprise. Nothing could beat the last surprise he'd had for her, but he didn't think that Thelma could take another one of such magnitude. Covering her eyes, he led her into the living room. When he dropped his hands, she opened her eyes to see before her a beautiful new rocking chair. It was an overstuffed, fabric-covered chair with maple arms and matching ottoman. "Try it out," he told her, and she sat, closing her eyes, and rocked momentarily. "I have a feeling that you'll be spending a lot of time in that chair, Mama," he proudly declared.

"Yes, Daddy, I believe you are right about that," Thelma agreed. With joyous anticipation in their faces, they left for the station.

CHAPTER 12

The Call

Charles had just showered and was getting ready to go out the door to work when the phone rang. Expecting Thelma to be on the other end of the line with such an early call, as she had called each morning of the two weeks since she had left, he picked up and greeted, "Good morning, little mama."

The voice on the other end remained silent for a moment before saying, "Hello. Is this Mr. Charles Howell?"

"Yes, this is Charles Howell."

"This is Gwendolyn from the law office of James Kirby in San Francisco."

"Yes, Gwendolyn. What can I do for you?"

"Well, Mr. Howell, you can get up here as soon as possible. Your baby girl arrived at 12:15 this morning, June 23, 1956. She's a whopping five pounds fifteen and a half ounces with lots of brown hair and a good, strong cry. All is well!"

He couldn't believe what he was hearing. He had to sit down for the rest of the news. "She'll be ready to leave the hospital in two days, so make your arrangements, and come get her."

Their baby girl was here at last! All the months of waiting and wondering were finally over. A girl—they had a little daughter. After a jump in the air, a clap of his hands, and a couple of deep breaths, he was ready to make his own call. As he dialed his parents' number, he thought of how he would tell Thelma. After one ring, two rings, three rings, "Hello," his mother cheerfully answered when she picked up the phone.

"Good morning, Mom. May I speak to my wife?"

"I'll go get her, Charles." He could hear her set down the phone and call, "Thelma, Charles is on the phone."

After what seemed to him like an eternity, she answered, "Good morning, honey. You're calling bright and early."

"Yes, I am," he told her. "I couldn't wait another minute! Rocky Road"—after his favorite ice cream flavor—"is here!"

"What? What did you say, honey?"

"I said that Rocky Road is here!"

"Our baby? Our baby has arrived? It's a boy?"

"No, honey, I just had to tease you a little! We have a little girl, and she's waiting for us to come take her home. I'll be ready to leave here in a few minutes just as soon as I let work know, and I'll be there late this afternoon. We'll go on to San Francisco in the morning."

"Oh, can it possibly be true? Is this really happening to us?"

"Yes, dear, it is. Our baby is here!"

"Okay, honey. Don't forget to get the diaper bag and the extra suitcase that is sitting beside it."

"They're already in the car. Bye-bye. I'll see you about four this afternoon."

"Drive safely, Charles."

By the time they ended their call, Grandpa Howell had already gone out the door to the hardware store to get the pink paint for the bassinet.

CHAPTER 13

Meeting Their Princess

Mile markers flew by as Charles made his way toward Fresno. During the drive, he began to reflect on this journey that he had started nearly six months ago. It had been a dream, kind of like betting on a horse race—not knowing whether he'd win or lose but betting on a hunch, hoping that his horse would come in first. So many things could have gone wrong: she could have lost the baby; she could have changed her mind; the baby could have been born with some defect. Any number of scenarios could have occurred, but luck had been with them. No, God had been with them! Only God could have blessed them with this miracle. Now, Charles wasn't really a religious man, but there are some things that one knows and just doesn't question. Yes, this Kathleen Terrell had provided the body for this special little girl, but this baby was and had always been theirs.

Just a couple of hours more until he reached his destination and could hold his beautiful wife in his arms. Could they wait the few hours left until they ascended the steps of St. Joseph's Hospital and beheld their baby girl for the very first time? Would she be their Nancy Caroline Howell after her great-grandmother, or would she look more like Suzanne, their little Su-Su? It all remained a dream until they held her, touched her, and kissed her little cheek.

Charles made good time and pulled into his parents' driveway at just after three in the afternoon. Thelma and his mom, Aline, wasted no time running out the front door to greet him. Thelma jumped into his arms, and his mom patted him on the back, greeting him with "Congratulations! We're so happy to have another little granddaughter to love and spoil!"

Thelma questioned while wringing her hands, "Are you sure that we shouldn't go on now to San Francisco, just to be sure that we're on time? I don't want to take any chances on being late, on making them think that we might have changed our minds!"

Charles assured her that they would leave at first light in the morning and arrive in plenty of time to get their little princess. "Besides, if my nose isn't deceiving me, Mom has cooked a celebratory feast of fried chicken, mashed potatoes and gravy, biscuits, fresh corn on the cob, and a lemon meringue pie. We can't let all of that go to waste, can we?"

Aline chimed in. "No, we can't! It's all ready, so let's sit down and eat while Charles tells us all the details!" Exhilaration was almost palpable in the room as they sat down to eat.

Once again, Charles went over everything that he'd been told since he received the phone call earlier that morning. "She was born at 12:15 this morning, has lots of curly brown hair and a strong cry. She weighs five pounds fifteen and a half ounces—"

"That's so small," Aline interrupted. "My lands, she'll look like a little picked bird. I bet we'll be able to bathe her in the mixing bowl!"

Now, Thelma started in. "Did they say how long she is and what color her eyes are? How about the delivery? Did they say how long it took for her to get here? Did they count her fingers and her toes?"

With his mouth full of biscuit, Charles laughed while shaking his head no. "I have told you everything that I know. I was too excited to ask any of those questions, but we'll know the answers to all of those very soon!"

Charles Sr. then put in his two cents. "My goodness, no one is going to be doing any sleeping tonight, so I might as well call Bobby and Tommy to come over for an all-night poker game!"

"No poker games tonight! Even if we don't sleep much, Charles and Thelma have a long drive tomorrow to San Francisco and back with that new baby! I don't want any excuses for them not to get back here for dinner tomorrow!" Aline warned.

There was no lack of excitement in the Howell home that evening. Aline, Bea, and Helen, daughter and daughter-in-law, had planned a little baby shower for Thelma and the new baby to be held the following evening. Since they now knew it was a baby girl, everything would be pink. Helen had several little brand-new dresses that Missy, just a year old, had never worn. Pammy, nine years old, was beside herself to have another girl cousin, and Mike was beside himself that he was the only boy. Oh, what a joyous time they would have in less than twenty-four hours!

With little sleep but high on adrenaline, Charles and Thelma took to the road at 5:30 a.m. Aline had wanted to prepare breakfast before they left, but Charles insisted that they'd be fine, and they were out the door. As they got farther north, the air cooled down some, which came as a relief to both of them. So often, the Bay Area was overcast, but that was not the case on this fine morning. The sun shone brightly, birds were singing, flowers were blooming, and Charles and Thelma were about to become parents!

They had made good time with little traffic, so Charles and Thelma decided to stop at a diner to get some breakfast and to change into their Sunday best. What does one wear to go meet a little princess for the very first time? They didn't know. The baby wouldn't know, but this was going to be the most special occasion of their lives; they needed to dress like it! After eating, Charles got their clothes out of the car, and they entered their respective restrooms to prepare to meet their little one. Thelma put on a lovely pastel pink shirtwaist dress with white high heels, checking her makeup one last time, and Charles was even wearing a tie when they exited the restrooms.

Back on the road, they were only a few miles from the city now. The highway ascended, and as they reached the summit, they could see the famous bridge in the distance. St. Joseph's Hospital was supposed to be easy to spot because it was a big white building on a hill. Even so, they drove around for quite a while with no hospital in sight. Charles pulled into a service station and got more specific directions to their destination from the attendant.

Once they pulled up to the curb in front of the hospital, Charles got out first, grabbed the diaper bag, and opened the door for Thelma. He took her hand to help her out of the car, and for just a moment, they looked into each other's eyes, for the very last time as a barren couple. When they left the hospital, finally, after eighteen years of marriage, they would be a family!

Entering the hospital, they were directed to an information desk. Charles told the woman their names and why they were there. In the sweetest, most congenial Southern accent, the attendant answered, "We have been expecting you, Mr. and Mrs. Howell. Come right this way." Charles and Thelma smiled at each other at her Southern twang. They already felt right at home.

Next, they were taken into a little room that must have been off the nursery, because they could hear various little cries coming from nearby. The door attached to the nursery then began to open, and a nurse entered with a tiny baby in her arms. The baby was wrapped in a pink flannel blanket, but all that they could really see was the top of her head, which indeed was covered with lots of brown curly hair. "Mr. Howell? I believe this baby girl belongs to you," the nurse announced as she placed the infant in his arms. He, in turn, lifted the baby to give her the gentlest of kisses on her forehead and placed their baby girl in her mother's arms. It was love at first sight!

The nurse gave them a few instructions and brought them a new-parent kit that contained bottles and formula. The bottles had already been sterilized and were ready for use. She also handed them a copy of Dr. Benjamin Spock's book, *Baby and Child Care.* "We understand that you live in a small town, so this will help out with anything you're not sure about—so you aren't running to the doctor too often!" she further instructed. Charles noticed Thelma chuckling to herself, as she had already read that book cover to cover several times. "I'll leave you alone now to greet your baby and to dress her in her going-home clothes. She has just a diaper and T-shirt on, which you may take with you."

Alone at last with their little princess, they opened the blanket and saw her precious little face—her creamy white complexion, turned-up nose, little rosebud lips, and long brown eyelashes. Charles and Thelma gasped at the beauty that lay before them. Farther down, they noticed her long fingers, perfect for playing the piano, and there were ten of them! Her legs were so tiny, and her little feet would need to grow quite a bit to fit into her only pair of shoes so far, the red cowboy boots. Just to make sure, they counted all ten toes as well, soon to become little piggies.

<hr />

Thelma picked the baby up and cradled her in her arms to smell her new-baby scent; she had smelled it on the various nieces and nephews but never on her own baby before. It was just as it should be. With tears flowing down her cheeks, she first thanked God, then her husband, and finally the woman who had given them this most precious gift. Dressing the baby in a light cotton floral dress and booties and wrapping her back in her pink blanket, Thelma sat down in a chair, while Charles signed the paperwork necessary for them to leave with their baby girl.

"Thelma, this is for the birth certificate. We need to know her name before we can leave. Is it Nancy or Suzanne?"

Just like that, she answered, "I think Suzanne is perfect for her. Hopefully, Great-Grandma will understand."

"Su-Su, it is! She'll have to!" Charles assured her and concurred.

"Are you ready?" the nurse questioned.

Thelma looked to Charles as he puffed out his chest and looked a little taller and proudly returned, "We've been ready our whole lives!"

"Oh, Mr. and Mrs. Howell, this beautiful vase of pink roses is from Mr. Kirby's office for you!" The nurse motioned to the corner table.

"Those are so lovely, but we have quite a way to travel to get home; I'm afraid that we'll need to leave them here. You know, if the birth mother is still here, could you give them to her, along with this card?" Thelma stated as Charles pulled the envelope out of his jacket pocket.

"I will see to that for you," the nurse replied. "Wait just a minute, please, and you'll be on your way."

CHAPTER 14

Family Approval

After insisting on carrying little Su-Su to the car, the nurse then handed her to Thelma, who had gotten into the back seat next to a travel bed for the baby. After she wished them a wonderful journey, the nurse closed the door as Thelma placed Suzanne, such a big name for such a tiny one, into the white wicker bed with a mattress wrapped in a pink cotton sheet. The bed had a hood, which she then pulled into place to keep the sun off the baby's face. Charles had observed the entire process, and when he could see that she was finished, he started the car; they were on their way.

Now the early afternoon, this day was even more magnificent than in the morning when they'd started out, though that seemed like a lifetime ago. Everything had changed. They saw the world differently now. Not only were they wearing rose-colored glasses; they also had protective lenses. Every few minutes, Charles would query, "How are you two doing back there? Do you need anything? Is the airflow okay? You don't think it's too hot, do you?" Thelma would let him know that all was well with a shake of her head and a radiant smile that didn't cease.

Through his rearview mirror, Charles glanced back often as Thelma watched every little move and breath that the baby made, attentive to her every need. Su-Su was sleeping soundly, but soon, she'd wake up hungry and need to be changed. He could hear Thelma digging into the diaper bag as she readied the supplies they would need: a changing pad, a diaper, a washcloth, the cute little duckling safety pins, the thermos of water, one of the bottles the hospital had given them, a bottle of formula, and a bib. Now, they just needed the baby to wake up!

Soon enough, almost on cue, Su-Su began to squirm and to make fussing sounds, and upon hearing them, Charles peered once again at Thelma through the rearview mirror as she picked up her newborn to really snuggle for the first time. What a beautiful scene it was to see his lovely wife holding her own baby daughter, no longer just a dream. Charles asked Thelma if she wanted to stop to take care of the baby's needs, but they decided to keep on the road so that they'd still have airflow. As they were nearing Fresno, the temperature had begun to rise, and they worried that it might get too hot for the baby.

Diaper change complete and bottle nearly drained along with two little burps, Su-Su was ready for the last leg of the trip to meet her new family. Already, the family had gathered to prepare the impromptu baby shower and celebratory meal to follow. Grandma and Grandpa Howell; Bea and Tom; Bob and Helen; and the three cousins, Pam, Mike, and Missy, were ready and waiting to meet this new little angel. At about four in the afternoon, Charles pulled up in front of his parents' home, and within just a few seconds, all the relatives were lined up outside the back door of the car, waiting for Thelma to open it. As she did, they yelled, "Congratulations! Welcome home, Su-Su!" Everyone was gleeful, and all the women were tearing up as they watched Thelma cradle her new baby in her arms and walk gently up to the door of the house.

All the smells were tantalizing but could not be rivaled by the beauty of the scene. Everywhere they looked, Charles and Thelma saw pink—pink balloons, pink flowers, pink pinwheel sandwiches, pink lemonade, and a pink cake. Additionally, Grandma Howell had prepared a ham, a big bowl of potato salad, deviled eggs, and a vegetable platter. Presents were stacked on the coffee table in the living room. It was certainly a welcoming sight prepared by a loving family!

Pam was the first to sit down on the couch and clearly announced, "I'm first to hold Su-Su!" Everyone laughed and looked at Thelma, who was still clutching her brand-new child for dear life. Thelma really wasn't ready to share her baby just yet, but she knew that she needed to. She wanted all to love and accept this newest family member, and just as her sisters-in-law had always done with her, she placed the baby in Pammy's arms. A united *aw* could be heard as all adored little Su-Su in her oldest cousin's arms.

Of course, the first diaper change at Grandma's house was a spectator event! On closer inspection, everyone could see how truly tiny this new baby girl was. Grandma couldn't stop commenting, "She looks like a little picked bird! She'll fit in my mixing bowl!" Aunt Bea explained to Pam how one takes care of the umbilical cord stub until it falls off. Thelma and Helen noticed that Su-Su had some heat rash from the short trip from San Francisco to Fresno, and they applied a little cornstarch. With the baby all set, they moved back to the living room so they could continue to pass the baby around while presents were opened.

Grandma was honored to feed Su-Su her bottle, and Bea got in line to do the burping. Pam helped with the presents as all kinds of little pink frilly dresses, blankets, nighties, booties, and hats were unfurled. Goodness, this little girl was set for the next few months of her life! After giving up the baby to Bea, Grandma cut the cake and passed around plates along with cups of pink lemonade. The men all sat together, talking of work and other manly topics, but Chuck had made sure to select a front-row seat for the festivities.

When all the gifts had been opened and everyone was full, cleanup began, and individual families prepared to say good-bye. It would be six months before they saw that new baby again, at Christmastime, and she was going to be so grownup by then, cooing and smiling. Hugs and kisses all around, and everyone was out the door.

Charles and Thelma surveyed the gifts and sat down to rest and to gaze upon their baby, content and happily sleeping in her grandmother's arms. While they reflected, Thelma brought up the heat rash, and Charles suggested that he send Thelma and Su-Su home on the bus while he drove the car home behind them. Summertime travel from Fresno to Kingman was not friendly to anyone, let alone a newborn baby. The bus would provide air conditioning and ward off any further heat rash development.

All decided, Charles called the bus station and bought two seats so that Thelma would have plenty of room to care for Su-Su. They would leave on a 9:00 a.m. bus, so Grandma indeed had time to bathe the baby in her mixing bowl before Chuck and Thelma had to leave for the station. Grandma was already lamenting their departure and being away from the baby so long. Grandpa assured her that he could probably get her down to Kingman for a visit while he traveled for business before the end of summer. Grandpa's promise helped quell those emotions.

The next morning, Charles, Thelma, and baby began the long journey home. On the way to the station, Charles and Thelma talked about their first night with Su-Su and were surprised that it had gone so smoothly. They had easily handled the feedings at 2:00 and 6:00 a.m. even though they were pretty tired from the travel, the party, and all the emotions of the day. Su-Su must have been tired too, from all the travel and holding. This trip to Kingman would be the true test of whether their little girl was a good traveler. Charles and Thelma knew that they could do it, though, and were happy at the thought that they'd be home for a while once they arrived.

PART III

Truth Revealed

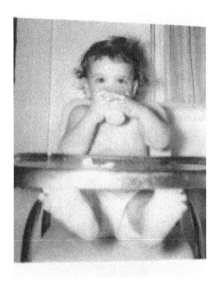

Through their tender care and nurturing,
A child's heart was won.
With stable patterns of living,
Trust and loyalty had begun.
Dedication to a purpose,
The gentle love they had to share
Surrounded by their wings spread wide,
I knew would always be there.

CHAPTER 15

What Is Adoption?

I was four years old when I first heard the word *adoption*. My cousin Mike locked me in a bedroom at my aunt and uncle's house in Fresno and taunted, "You're not even a real member of our family!" Hearing my cries, my mother burst into the room and took me in her arms to comfort me. I don't remember what she said to console me, but I do remember feeling that everything was okay. I did not suffer an identity crisis due to Mike's hurtful jeers.

The word did not find meaning for me again until the first day of third grade in Las Vegas. My teacher, Miss Jones, asked the students about their family circumstances as an introductory activity and told us to raise our hands if the situations she mentioned applied to us. She asked who had brothers and sisters, who was the youngest or the oldest child in the family, and who was a middle child. Last, she asked who was adopted. I remember looking around the room and seeing three hands begin to rise in the air. Slowly, cautiously, I raised my hand too. I wasn't quite certain what the term meant, but I knew that somehow it applied to me. Miss Jones then stressed the words that would make all the difference in my life. She explained, "Do you know that you were the most wanted of all?"

That dear, blessed woman—I'm sure that she didn't know what

an impact she had made on my life that day! I still wasn't sure what *adopted* meant, but I knew that it was an okay thing to be; after all, my teacher had said so. For the next four-plus years, I was content with the knowledge that I had about my life, but then at the age of thirteen, I did suffer a short-lived, but nevertheless significant, identity crisis. Along with questions about God and the purpose of life, I often wondered about my beginnings. I started asking myself such questions as these: *Why was I given up for adoption? Didn't they want me? Do I have brothers and sisters somewhere?* and *What would my life have been like if I hadn't been adopted?* However, I never gave utterance to these questions. I never asked my mom and dad for the answers. I was afraid to. I didn't want them to think that I didn't love them or that I was ungrateful for the life they had given me. They had always been wonderful parents, the very best! I didn't want for anything in my life, and though kids would often say, "You must be a spoiled brat because you're an only child," I knew the truth was that I was not spoiled but loved.

For my thirteenth birthday, I had a slumber party. Several of my closest friends stayed over for the night, and we waited up until past midnight to greet the dawning of June 23. Amid the fun and laughter, someone asked the question, "What time were you born?" *What time was I born?* I had no idea.

I asked my mother the same question, and she led me to her bedroom. There in the cedar chest, underneath fine linen and homemade crocheted doilies that smelled strongly of cedar, lay an envelope. She exhumed the envelope from the chest, and inside it, I saw what appeared to be important documents. Among those documents was my birth certificate. It was the first time I had ever seen it, and I studied it in amazement, searching every detail. This rather small piece of paper contained the state's official seal. It said that I was born at 12:15 a.m. My mother's name was Thelma Blanche Morrisett Howell, and my father's name was Charles Edward Howell Jr. I was born in San Francisco, California, at St. Joseph's Hospital. It surprised me that such a small document could tell so much.

Seeing no sign of another mother or father on the certificate, I braved the question, "Do you know anything about the people that had me?"

My mother looked at me in all seriousness and simply stated, "No, we don't know anything about that. They just called us and said that you were ours, and we went to get you." Now, this was my mother speaking. Mothers always speak the truth. They didn't know anything, and there was nothing more to ask. Twenty-three years passed before I was to learn the next part of the story.

During those teen years, I lived my life as most teenagers do: spending a great deal of time with friends, having sleepovers, hanging out at each other's homes, riding bikes, shopping at the mall, and going horseback riding. And I kept myself greatly occupied with dance lessons, school sports, and Honor Society, and doing well on my schoolwork. Holidays were always extra special at our house, especially Christmas, where my mom went all out with decorations, and we put up a tree; made yummy fudge, divinity, and date roll; and constantly played Christmas music on the stereo. I remember lying on the carpet by the tree at night, with only the tree lights on, listening to the music and cuddling my dogs, Daisy and Suzette.

A few days before Christmas, Mom would go into her bedroom, not to be disturbed while she wrapped the gifts that my parents had for me, and then every so often, she would come out with a stack to place under the tree. I was not allowed to touch or shake the presents! The excitement steadily built up to Christmas morning, which was always the very best time of all. I wasn't allowed to come out of my room until my dad had the movie camera ready to capture my surprise at what

Santa had brought. That finished, we would sit down around the tree and open all the presents. There was always a good amount, but in our family, we also wrapped things like socks, hankies, and underwear, which were due to be replaced!

At fifteen and a half, I began to date the young man who would someday become my husband. Add dating to an already-busy schedule, and I didn't have much time left to breathe, let alone time to get into any trouble. Mom and Dad always agreed that I had been such a good girl, so easy to raise. Part of that was due to the fact that I never wanted to do anything that would make them feel disappointed in me or love me any less. I'm not sure if all children feel that way or if it is just the grateful, adopted ones! I graduated valedictorian and married my sweetheart right after high school, so we started college together as newlyweds.

CHAPTER 16

Daddy's Revelation

At thirty-six, I was a busy mother of four. My children were my life, and I stayed busy morning through night trying to keep up with the housework, the laundry, and their numerous activities. It was a joyous time. I loved my roles as mother and wife and all that went with them: I was a PTA mom, a leader for Weight Watchers, a school aide at the kids' elementary school, an active member in my church, and a part-time puppy breeder. During this time, my father had been battling lymphoma, a cancer that had settled mostly in his digestive tract. He had been in and out of remission four times in the eight years since his diagnosis, and we were used to the side effects of his treatments, which made him so ill. We were also always a little on edge for fear that the cancer might come back in full force to plague him again.

I was accustomed to taking the children to school and then coming home to do my housework in the early morning hours. When I needed a break, I'd sit down for a minute to call my mom and dad to see how they were doing. Mom was working in new accounts at a bank, but Dad had needed to retire early in order to take his treatments. One particular fall morning in October 1988, I had gotten the last load of wash in the dryer when I decided to make my morning call. Dad answered the phone, and he sounded a little different than usual. As I think back on it now, it seemed as if he was under the influence of pain medication. He spoke slowly and sounded kind of mellow, almost as if he were in a dreamlike state.

After the usual small talk, he began to tell me a story. It somewhat confused me, as I didn't know what he was getting at. Within a few minutes, it became clear that he was talking about me, about my adoption. I had been waiting all my life to hear this story, yet switching from what had been my truth for so long, that my parents didn't know anything about the birth family, was not an easy transition for my mind to make. Sitting statue-like on a barstool, I listened intently, afraid to miss any detail.

Daddy told me how he had arranged my adoption before I was born, when my birth mother was still early in the pregnancy. He told me that I had two brothers he knew of, about four and five years older than me. I was the most surprised when he told me that he had seen her and the younger of my two brothers. My interest immediately jumped to what he remembered about this woman who had given me life. She was an attractive woman, he said, a little taller than me, about five-foot-six, with brown hair and brown eyes. There was a definite resemblance between her and me; I had her lips and hips, two of my most distinguishing features.

The story then began to change as he told me how she held up the adoption because she tried to get me back. When, at my six-month mark, my parents went to court to finalize the adoption, imagine their shock when the judge came in and told them that the birth mother was there. My parents already had bags packed, prepared to leave their current lives behind and flee to Mexico if the court did not rule in their favor. She had filed a petition to regain custody of me, which held up the adoption for another year. Apparently, my birth mother had remarried and now felt that she could properly care for me. She had never wanted to give me up, and she intended to get me back.

This became the most torturous year of my parents' lives. Welfare visitations continued to make sure that my placement in Charles and Thelma's home was the best choice for me. After that year, when my parents returned to court, Kathleen was there, with her son Steven. The night before the court date, she had decided to go see a priest. She told him the story of her little girl, and when she was through, the priest advised her to leave me with my adoptive parents. He stressed to her that I knew these people as my parents by this time and that she already had two other children and the ability to have others if she wished. My birth parents would never have any other children.

That day at court, my father saw her. She was sitting with Steven on a bench in the hallway outside the courtroom. Though they did not meet face-to-face, he saw her well enough to be able to describe her. I would find out later that Kathleen, too, had seen Thelma holding me, and when she saw this mother with desperation in her eyes, she knew that she couldn't go through with it. She wrote a note to Charles and Thelma, which she left with the court clerk, telling them about her meeting with the priest and her change of heart. She said she would never bother them again, and she left.

Needless to say, I was in shock after learning all this information. My dad and I got off the phone, and I grabbed the nearest piece of paper that I could find and wrote down all that he had told me. I didn't know my birth parents' names, but at that point, it really didn't matter. After all those years, I finally knew something about the circumstances of my adoption. It felt like a fairy tale to me—meat for a novel made for television. I had gained some of the missing pieces, and I was elated to have this history.

Three months later, the day after Christmas of 1988, my father was hospitalized. Along with the lymphoma, he had now developed acute leukemia, and he was not expected to live long. During his last two and a half weeks, I spent most of my time at the hospital. We brought the kids in one evening to celebrate Mom and Dad's fifty-first wedding anniversary, and old friends came to say good-bye. On January 13, 1989, my father left his earthly existence. He was only sixty-eight years old, and I felt robbed to lose him so early. However, at the same time, I felt extremely grateful to have had such a wonderful father. He had been watching over me since before I was born, and I was certain that not even death could keep him from continuing his vigil.

CHAPTER 17

Mama's Guilt

Along with the tremendous sadness that accompanies losing those we love, an overwhelming feeling of gratitude permeated my being, which provided immeasurable peace. Telling me my story just a few months before his passing, Daddy helped cushion the blow. He knew that it would; that's why he told me. It explained a depth of love that I had never really understood. It actually propelled me along so that I could plan his funeral, sing at it, and even give his eulogy. My mother was alone now, and I was left to watch over her. I needed to be strong, as Daddy's example had taught me to be.

Mama did unbelievably well for almost a year after Daddy's passing. She carried on with her lady friends: going out to dinner, participating in a singing group that performed at her Eastern Star and Daughters of the Nile functions, and attending Sunday church service with them, and coming out to our house most Sundays for dinner kept her life busy and full. However, around the one-year anniversary of Daddy's death, I received a frightening call from one of her friends that my mom had collapsed while they were having lunch. An ambulance was called, and the paramedics checked her out, finding that she had experienced a panic attack and had hyperventilated. Her friend was able to drive her home, but the paramedics advised that she see her doctor right away. We saw the doctor that very afternoon, and the doctor came to the conclusion that Mama had reacted badly to anesthesia from when she had knee surgery, which had subsequently caused her to become depressed and start having the panic attacks. With new medicine and knowledge of how to deal with hyperventilation, we were able to get her feeling right again so she could positively navigate life without my dad.

In 2003, Mama was diagnosed with breast cancer. Her earlier scare right before my birth had been allayed with the diagnosis of a benign cyst. But in the years that followed, doctors had left her on hormones too long, and estrogen had induced the cancer. Since the tumor was so small, about one centimeter, or the size of a pea, and it didn't seem to have spread, her doctor advised a lumpectomy.

We had been inadequately prepared for this day's surgery ordeal. The pain it caused her and the amount of drainage from the surgery site were truly frightening. I stayed with her for several nights, and the kids took turns staying with her for several weeks afterward. When her stitches were removed, the doctor further advised we arrange a chemotherapy regimen with an oncologist. We discovered these treatments might last several years, with checkups every six months to make sure the cancer was still in check.

Though Mama's cancer was nothing like the types that Daddy had succumbed to, in her mind, cancer was a death sentence, ready to pounce at any time it well pleased. With this on her mind, she felt compelled to speak to me. One day, Mama called and said that she needed to talk. This was not to be one of our regular check-in-every-other-day conversations. Fearing bad news regarding her breast cancer prognosis, I tried to prepare myself for our discussion. I went over to her house the next afternoon, a couple of hours before I would need to pick up the kids from school.

She began by saying, "There is something that I have been thinking a lot about lately. I feel like I am being selfish keeping it to myself any longer. So many of our family members are gone now, and when I'm gone, you won't have much family left." This made me terribly perplexed and afraid. I couldn't imagine what she was about to reveal to me in this conversation, and I was beginning to feel not nearly prepared enough to hear it.

And then she declared, "I know more about your birth family than your daddy told you before he died, and I need to tell you so that you can find them." This announcement was the last thing that I expected to hear. I really had not given the idea of finding my birth family a thought since my father's revelation before his death. In fact, Mama and I had never spoken of that conversation. What I did know had satisfied my yearning for about fifteen years, but then I began to wonder why that was. I supposed that it was because I had a mother. That place was already filled in my life. To know that my birth mom had wanted me and had tried to get me back had made me feel more secure in my position as an adopted child, and my life was extremely busy with beginning my teaching career and raising my family. In the back of my mind, though, part of me still needed to know my humble beginnings; I still needed to know my true identity.

As Mom began to tell me what she knew, it surprised me to learn my birth mother's name, her place of origin, and the fact that her brother was a police officer in her town. The last fact seemed the most logical way to try to contact her, aside from getting a phone book from the town and calling all of those with the same last name. As I discussed these options with Mom, she suddenly remembered that my birth uncle had died in an accident. She had read about this in a newspaper years earlier.

Something was bothering me as she revealed all that she knew. Why had she always told me that she knew nothing about my birth family? I had to give utterance to this thought, so I asked. She took a deep breath and then explained that it had taken her a long time to get over the fear of possibly losing me. "When she decided to withdraw her petition, the judge told us that you were ours and that we needed to forget that this had happened, to go on and live our lives without fear. That's what we tried to do."

I couldn't fault my mother for keeping this information from me. She had tried to put that fear of losing me behind her, but she had never been able to truly do that. I honestly can't say that I would have done anything differently than she did. As the recipient of the information, I felt both excited and hesitant—excited to finally know the complete truth but hesitant at how the truth might change my life and those I loved.

CHAPTER 18

My Search Begins

It took me a few weeks to decide if it was the right time to try to find my birth family. I hesitated in part because I was getting ready to move up from teaching middle school to teaching high school and anticipated a greatly increased workload. However, the main reason I hesitated was because I had not told all my children of my adoption. My reasoning for this was because I never wanted my children to feel that my wonderful parents were not their "real" grandparents. Our eldest was now twenty-three, but we had three who were younger. I did still feel extremely protective of my parents' feelings and knew what a tremendous sacrifice my mom had made in telling me this additional information.

Once I decided that I'd make a start, I went to the public library and copied the pertinent pages of the phone book. I began my short-lived calling regimen once my children went off to school each day. Most often, no one answered the phone. Occasionally, I'd get an answering machine and leave a message. Only one of those messages was returned. The few I did catch at home said that they had no one in their family by that name. I found this process very discouraging and quite stressful. I did not have the time nor the fortitude to deal with the ineptitude of my research method right then. In less than a week of calls, my new hopes were dashed. Therefore, I decided to let the search go for the time being.

Though I wasn't actively pursuing my quest, it remained on my mind as I thought about other ways to find my birth family. My mother was now eighty-four, but I knew that my birth mother was six years younger, making her seventy-eight. The chances of her still being alive were not great but still conceivable. I did discover that most adoptions during that time period were done through Catholic Charities, and since my birth family was Catholic, I thought the church just might be able to provide the answer to my dilemma.

Catholic Charities proved somewhat helpful in providing basic adoption information that I did not know. For instance, they informed me that in most cases, adoptions were closed, and one could not open the records unless the birth family gave permission. Another issue was we did not know where the adoption proceedings had begun. We knew where the birth family was, but I had been born in a different part of the state, further complicating matters. In the end, they suggested that I contact the courts where my adoption had been finalized. This suggestion led to the golden ticket.

The courts were extremely helpful. In Mohave County, Arizona, they had a confidential intermediary program that did just what I needed at very little cost to me. I provided all the information that I knew, which wasn't much and some of it wrong, and they assigned my case to an individual who would research, open the records if found, and gain permission from the birth family for us to make contact. The woman assigned to my case truly was a Godsend. She was experienced, positive, and pleasant to work with. She was also empathetic to my situation and related emotions. In the end, it took her only three months to locate my birth family, but those three months were an emotional roller coaster.

She started with Catholic Charities but could not locate any records within that system. That could only mean that the adoption had been private and would probably be more difficult to find. We agreed to talk every two to three weeks, at which time she would report her leads and how they had turned out. It seemed that every lead she'd find would take her to a dead end. After several such conversations, I was becoming a wreck. I'd get my hopes up only to be disappointed again and again. Finally, I told her that I appreciated all that she was doing for me, but I had decided that I didn't want her to call me until she knew something concrete. This was the middle of summer of 1996.

CHAPTER 19

Birth Family Found

With my move up to high school in just a few weeks, I felt the need to reinforce my knowledge in teaching Shakespeare's plays. I had enrolled in a weeklong "Shakespeare for Teachers" course at Southern Utah University in Cedar City, Utah, in mid-July 1996. All the family came up with me to attend the Renaissance Feast and two plays. They then returned home, and I stayed to finish out the week in classes. This was before I had a cellular phone, so I would go to a pay phone to check in with my family. Following my last class of the day, before I had dinner and went back to my dorm for the night, I called home to make sure that my family had arrived safely.

After the phone rang several times, my exuberant eleven-year-old son answered. Out of breath, he exclaimed, "Mom, she called! She found your birth family!" My husband then came to the phone, confirming what my son had said and adding that the intermediary had called five days earlier, on the day we had left for Utah. He gave me the return phone number, and when we hung up, I looked around the entryway of the Walmart and tried to prepare myself for what was to be one of the most significant communications of my life.

Anxiously, I dialed the number and waited for the intermediary to answer. When she did, she stated that she'd been awaiting my call for several days. I told her where I was and that the family had just retrieved the message earlier in the day. I then heard her take a deep breath before she forewarned, "I want to prepare you by saying that these situations don't always have storybook endings. I have located your birth mother through your brother, Steven. She is in poor health and currently living with another brother and his family. You knew about your two older brothers, and she remarried and had three more boys after you. Suzanne, your brothers have always known that they had a sister somewhere. I have the number where she is staying if you'd like to call her now."

When she stopped talking, it was my cue to exhale. Dazed, I turned my purse upside down to find a pen and paper to jot down the number. My intermediary concluded, "I will send you all the data that I have gathered in a few days. I'd love to hear how your meeting goes."

As I slipped more coins into the slot and dialed the number she had given me, I really could not believe that this was actually happening. It was surreal—as surreal as the day that my dad had first told me the fairy tale!

One, two, three rings, and a pickup: "Hello?"

CHAPTER 20

Is It Really You?

"Hello. My name is Suzanne Fabbi, and I believe that my birth mother, Kathleen Terrell, is expecting my call." I could hear voices in the background, and then after what seemed like a lifetime, a woman's voice spoke into the receiver.

"Hello, is this my daughter? Is it really you? I didn't know if this day would ever come. I was hoping that it would, but it has been so long." As she finished, Kathleen began to cry. I, too, began crying.

I told her that I didn't want to upset her but that I had been told she wished to be in contact with me. Still crying, she handed the phone over to a man who identified himself as my brother. He told me again that they had always known they had a sister. "Our mother," he stated, "just got out of the hospital, and she's staying with us indefinitely while she goes through some rehabilitation and physical therapy. She isn't walking right now, and we live upstairs, which makes it hard for us to get her up and down and to the appointments she has. We do want to meet you, but you'll have to come to us. Is that possible?"

It would have to be a rushed trip, but I told him that I thought my husband, my youngest daughter, and I could come the next weekend just before I reported back to school. He gave me the names and numbers of my four other brothers, one of whom lived back east, and told me that they were expecting my call. Here I had been an only child for most of my life, and now, within a day, I was one of six children and the only girl! I had to pinch myself several times to make sure that this was me and that what was happening was real.

During the following week, I gathered copies of Christmas letters that I had sent out almost every year since my husband and I had children so that my birth mother and brothers could learn a bit about me and my family. My brothers were gaining two nieces and two nephews, and I was gaining six nephews and two nieces. Most I would meet in just a few days. As I had been raised an only child, I found the thought of having all this family almost impossible to comprehend. I had lived a relatively serene and orderly life thus far. Yes, I had raised four children. And I had two brothers-in-law and a sister-in-law, their spouses, and their children, but that was my husband's side of the family. Now, I was to meet my own family, blood relatives, to discern our similarities through our common genetics as well as our differences because of the nurturing that we had received from different parents.

The week dragged as I anticipated the meeting. I went to my new school to set up my room, took the kids school shopping, and tried hard not to assume anything, but thoughts of meeting my birth mother and so many brothers overwhelmed me: *How will I be greeted? Will my birth mom be happy with who I have become? Do I look like her now? Will my brothers and I look related since we have different fathers? Will we have anything in common? Will our meeting feel comfortable, or will it feel estranged?* These thoughts and many others incessantly swirled around in my head until I could only escape them by falling asleep, which was also challenging because I was experiencing insomnia, as I always did right before a new school year.

CHAPTER 21

Five-Star Visit

Within a day of the call, my husband and I had cleared our schedules and had planned a trip to meet my birth mother and possibly four of my five brothers. We left on Thursday afternoon when my husband got off work and arrived shortly before midnight. It hadn't occurred to us to make a hotel reservation before we left, but as it turned out, it was the weekend of a huge blues festival, which we had not anticipated. After stopping at a fifth hotel just to make sure it had no vacancies, we settled on a five-star accommodation in the center of downtown Monterey.

My youngest brother had expressed the most excitement about meeting me and had told me to call him as soon as we were in town. When we got settled in our room, though it was the wee hours of the morning, I called him as promised. I told him where we were staying, and he proclaimed that he'd arrive there in ten minutes. *Now?* I thought. In eight minutes, the knock aroused us from our travel-worn catnap!

Upon opening the door, I found myself swept up into the arms of a six-foot-something little brother, who twirled me around in circles. Hugs and kisses came next, as I then introduced him to my husband and his new niece. When the embraces ended, my brother and I stepped back for a moment and just looked at each other. Clearly, this was a once-in-a-lifetime event, one that neither of us would ever forget, but all that we could really summon was small talk. I'm pretty sure that I was in shock. After a few more minutes, he excused himself so that we could get some rest and told me to call him in the morning when I was ready to go see "Mom." She was back in the hospital.

I slept very little that night, though the bed was extremely plush and comfortable. I had too many thoughts flying through my head to manage to settle down. I had felt a definite connection with my youngest brother, who had told me how different his life would have been had I been in it. I pictured him in a diaper and me holding him on my hip. I wondered what my other brothers were like and if I'd feel the same connection with them. When I could stay in bed no longer and the sun began to peek through the curtains, I got up and went in to shower. Today was the day that I would meet the woman who had given me life! This was unreal.

Once we were all ready for the day, I called my brother, and within a few minutes, we were off to breakfast. He had called the other brothers to let them know that we would head to the hospital right before noon. It would take until then for the hospital staff to get our mother up and dressed. Only my little family and my youngest brother would be there for our first visit.

It wasn't quite clear to me why Kathleen had gone back to the hospital until my brother pressed the elevator button and informed us that we were going to the psychiatric ward. Apparently, finding out about me had thrown her into another bout with manic depression. That knowledge broke my heart, but my brother tried to comfort me by saying not to feel too badly because she spent a lot of time there. That made me wonder what we'd find.

The elevator doors opened into a small reception area with a few chairs and small vinyl and metal couches. On the far side of the area appeared to be a nurses' station, which was encased in glass from floor to ceiling with a small open window. Several patients were sitting in the area, most wearing hospital gowns, some alert, and others apparently napping. My brother went over to the window to check in and then proceeded over to a silver-haired woman who was asleep in a wheelchair. This woman was my birth mother. As he began whispering in her ear, he motioned for me, my husband, and my daughter to come over where he was. Getting closer, I could hear him saying, "Mom, wake up! Your daughter is here. Your baby girl is here."

Kathleen was so sleepy, in a drug-induced sleep, and though she tried really hard to wake up, she just couldn't. I found it a little disappointing, though understandable, but the situation made my brother quite upset. He left our mother's side and went back to the nurses' station, where, as I later found out, he expressed his displeasure at Mom's being so drugged when she was to meet her daughter for the first time since babyhood. He further expressed that we would come back the next day, and he expected that she would be coherent.

The next day, we were joined at the hospital by my two older brothers, Steven and Michael, and Michael's girlfriend. This time, when the elevator doors opened, Kathleen was dressed, wearing some makeup, and quite alert. Her chair was positioned so that she'd see us the minute we stepped out. Her eyes opened wide, as in surprise, and a beautiful smile adorned her face. As I walked toward her, she extended her arms out to me, and I walked into them. She lay her head against me, holding on for dear life, and I leaned down so that my head rested on hers. We stayed that way for what seemed like forty years as she wept tears of happiness. When our embrace loosened a bit, I stood up and pulled my husband and daughter over to meet her. Then my three brothers joined the reunion circle. All our faces wore smiles at the occasion of our newfound family. We all sat down in the reception area, talking and laughing, my brothers sharing stories of childhood and adding how different it would have been with their sister there.

Kathleen then announced that she had some things she needed to tell me. "I do know who your father is, Suzanne. His name is Richard Ross. He wasn't married but didn't want to marry me. You see, I always thought that when a man smiled at me and was nice to me, he was in love with me. You know, I did try to get you back. Richard gave me the money for the train fare, but when I saw that poor mother, I just couldn't go through with it." I told her that I had been blessed with a very good life, and I thanked her for giving me life. Before we left for the day, my daughter and I sang a song titled "You're Not Alone," and there wasn't a dry eye left when we departed.

That evening, the fourth of my five brothers and his wife and two sons, along with the others, joined us at a popular pizza parlor, where we all got acquainted, ate heartily, and, truth be known, stared at each other. I'm sure that we were thinking the same things: them thinking, *How did we grow up without this sister?* and me thinking my life would have been *so* different growing up with all these brothers!

Michael, my eldest brother, brought along old pictures that he wanted to gift me with, which provided me with a bit more family history. There were pictures of Kathleen as a baby, as a teen, as a new bride, and with the love of her life who went off to war. There were pictures of her with her sister, just eighteen months younger, in her drum majorette outfit and boots, not unlike my own red boots. Michael detailed the story of how Kathleen's sweetheart went off to war and how her sister was about to announce her engagement to her boyfriend. He said that Kathleen couldn't stand the idea that her younger sister would marry first, and she managed to find her own beau so she could announce her own engagement the same day. This was Michael's father, who left her and Michael when he was just seven days old. These stories helped me better understand her manic depression and the actions that had complicated her life and caused her and others so much pain.

Before I returned to Las Vegas and my real-life responsibilities, my four brothers, my husband, my daughter, and I ate one more meal together at the local Sizzler steak house. For this farewell meal, I pulled out my wedding album, in which my brothers viewed pictures of the parents who had raised me, becoming more familiar with their sister and her life that was so foreign to them. Michael handed me a notebook of poetry that he had written, including one very special entry just composed about his long-lost but finally found sister. This gift touched me to tears. After hugs all around, we said good-bye with a promise to return to celebrate our birthdays, four of which were in June, the following summer.

The long drive home gave me time to absorb all that had happened and to start to settle into my role as sister—two brothers older than me, three younger than me, one of whom I'd yet to meet, not to mention other possible siblings from my birth father still to contact. One thing was certain: I was experiencing an extreme emotional high and a feeling of wholeness I'd never felt before, which allowed me to practically float the eight hours home! *Did that really happen?* I asked myself. *Have the stars finally aligned after forty years in our universe? What are the chances under such extreme circumstances? Was it meant to be? Yes!*

This trip had answered most of my questions about who I was, why I was given up for adoption, and the alternate life that I might have lived had I not been adopted. My birth family and I had lost so many years, but we still had the future and the hope that we could forge new relationships in the time that we still had left.

CHAPTER 22

So Many Brothers

The harsh buzzing of the alarm jerked me out of bed on a Monday morning. Gone were the pleasant dreams, replaced by the reality and excitement of starting a new school year at a new school. I had anticipated moving up to high school and was thrilled to be moving to a top school in our state. I didn't have much time to think about my monumental weekend, but it certainly didn't go far from the forefront of my mind.

On my way home from my first day back to work, I stopped at the store to select a photo album in which to place the new family photos that I had been given. Then in the evening, as I sat at the kitchen table with the pictures spread out before me, I couldn't help but reflect on all that I had experienced and learned. My birth family had lived difficult lives. My mother's mental illness had made them so. They had missed out on stability so much of their lives. Kathleen had almost died of a lithium overdose, and the older boys had to become caretakers of their younger brothers, in the '60s and '70s, each time their mother checked herself into the psychiatric ward. Her own mother and brother had tried to have her committed, and Kathleen had fought desperately to keep her family together.

As I began to place the pictures in the album, two of them stood out to me. One was of Michael and Steven, clearly at an age after my birth but with me missing. The other showed the two older boys with their new little brother, the one born just after me. Again, I was missing. Thoughts of how different my life would have been had I not been adopted once again flooded my mind. When I had given voice to that thought at our last dinner before departing the previous night, Michael had defended, "Yes, but you would have been loved." And I knew that; I had been wanted.

My first week back to school flew by, and as the weekend approached, thoughts of my birth father began to surface. Kathleen had suggested that I write to Richard Ross in care of his business, and she had further added, "He won't deny it!" This made me think of what goals I had for possibly meeting him. They differed slightly from those I had once had for meeting my birth mom. She, after all, had carried me for nine months and given birth to me. He, on the other hand, had tried to deny his paternity and left her to deal with the consequences of their actions by herself. She had tried to get me back. She had given birth to my five brothers. She wanted me in her life. I had no idea how he would react to the news that I knew who he was.

Certainly, I wanted medical information. I was interested to know if I had any other younger siblings. I would enjoy seeing pictures, and if possible, I desired to meet him. With these things in mind, I had a few pictures printed of me and my family and began my letter to Richard Ross. The letter wasn't long. I simply stated that I had found Kathleen and that she had named him as my father. I told him what I hoped to achieve and closed with my contact information. Stamped and mailed, the letter was on its way the next day. The ball was now in his court.

In the weeks that followed, I tried not to think too much about how my birth father had received my letter, though I anxiously checked the mail when I returned home from work each day. I was so busy dealing with my new job responsibilities and my children's beginning-of-school routines, coordinating all that had to be done to get everyone where they needed to go and home each day, that I didn't have too much idle time left to contemplate the next phase of my birth story. But every once in a while, the thought of whether he would embrace me or deny his part in my life managed to squeeze through.

CHAPTER 23

He Won't Deny It

With it being a new school year, the high school offered many in-service meetings to bring new teachers up to speed on the technology that we were expected to utilize. Two weeks into the year, the school offered an evening in-service meeting that I needed to attend. Because my new school was quite a distance from my home, I planned to stay after school to grade introductory essays until the meeting began.

About 7:00 p.m., we finished for the night, and just as I began to walk to my car, my phone rang. It was my husband, and he had some news for me. He had just gotten off the phone with my birth father's attorney. The attorney's purpose in calling was to "check me out," as my husband interpreted, to find out just what this phantom daughter wanted with his client. Mr. Webster had left his number and asked that I return his call that night if possible.

Mr. Webster really was a very nice man. He said that Richard had asked him to call me, that he had grown up with Richard and Kathleen, and that he intended to tell Richard that his daughter seemed like a lovely individual he should meet. With that, we disconnected, and within five minutes, my phone rang again. "Hello, Suzanne. This is Richard Ross. I understand that you've been in touch with Kathleen, and she told you that I'm your father." There it was. Already, I began to feel a denial coming on.

I answered, "Yes, she did! Do you want me to have testing done to be sure this is correct?"

Without hesitation, he assured, "No, Suzanne, that isn't necessary; you look just like my youngest son!"

Youngest son? At least two more brothers? I thought.

I was stunned by his admittance. He told me that he had been quite surprised to get my letter, that he hadn't thought that I'd ever be part of his life. He advised that his hearing was poor and that it was hard for him to talk on the phone because he wore hearing aids in both ears. He said he had also had a triple-bypass surgery in the 1970s, but it didn't slow him down. At seventy, he was still an avid skier, and he still hunted and fished as often as possible. He stated that he'd send some pictures to me and that he'd love to meet me; however, he had something that he needed to do first. He needed to tell his wife about me! They married two years after my birth, and he had never told her that he had a daughter. He ended by saying that he'd send me the pictures the next day and that he'd work on how to tell his wife.

Wow, I thought as I drove the rest of the way home, *this is starting to sound more and more like a soap opera!*

True to his word, Richard sent me a short letter that contained two pictures: one of him alone on a fishing boat and the other of him and his youngest son standing on a dock. He called again about a week later while on a hunting trip to Bishop, California. It was evening, and the connection was poor. He admitted that he still had not told his wife about me but that he would tell her soon. He also noted that he'd call me again when he got back home. I was beginning to feel hopeful that I'd meet my birth father in no time, and then I heard nothing more.

CHAPTER 24

Ultimatum

About a month later, Dick Webster called me to tell me what happened. Apparently, Richard had come up with a scheme to tell his wife, and it had backfired big time. He had called me from his office, knowing that his wife, who was also his office manager, would check over the telephone bill and ask whom he had called in Las Vegas. That's exactly what happened, but when he told her he had a daughter, she flipped out. He had deceived her for thirty-eight years, and she was going to divorce him if he had anything to do with me. Dick continued, "You see, Richard's wife was raised in a puritanical home, and she took this really hard."

No kidding! I thought. *This is 1996, not 1600 New England!*

Dick finished by stating that Richard had been excited to hear from me and really wanted to meet me, but he had to abide by his wife's mandate because he didn't want his marriage to end. Well, that was that! What else could be done?

It was my turn to express how I felt. I told Dick to please tell Richard that I was sorry that it had turned out this way. I told him that I didn't want to cause him any trouble, that I certainly didn't want his marriage to end. I would abide by his wishes, but my door would remain open if things should change. Finally, I advised that as long as Richard was alive, I would stay out of my brothers' lives, but after he passed, they would know that they had a sister. I guess I knew who wore the pants in the family!

I must admit I was disappointed that I wouldn't get to meet my birth father. He had been excited to meet me, to know his only daughter, but that wasn't to be. In all that had happened thus far, this marked the first time that I had felt like I was someone's dirty little secret.

Meanwhile, my birth mother and brothers were wasting no time making up for lost time. Kathleen and Michael had written. My youngest brother had called. I had talked with my brother who lived in New York and was emailing with Michael and responding to his writing. Before long, we had planned our June birthday party to celebrate the four of Kathleen's children born in that month.

My mom, Thelma, went through a period of adjusting to the new family that I had found. Though she had given me the information that had enabled me to find them, actually having them in my life was another matter. I can only imagine how hard it was for her when we'd leave town to go visit. We always invited her to come along, but she'd always say, "Maybe next time." However, when Richard's attorney told me that Richard would not be able to be part of my life, it raised my mother's hackles, and she was prepared to fight for her daughter. Pen in hand, she composed a ten-page letter extolling my many virtues, which she promptly sent off to Richard and Anne. Once again, she had demonstrated her devotion to me and my dignity. Their answer back was not what she wanted nor expected. In the least amount of words that could convey a message, they curtly replied, "We received your letter. Please don't contact us again."

One can only surmise Anne's reasoning in keeping me away from my birth father. Did she do it to save her dignity? Perhaps she did it out of insecurity. Maybe she did it to enact the severest form of punishment on Richard for his years of deception. I have a feeling that it was a combination of all these reasons, but ultimately, it probably had something to do with her fear that I'd try to lay claim to their fortune. It was never about that. I didn't need nor did I want their money, though I do have a legal right to it. So afraid that I might show up, she didn't even have a public funeral for Richard when he passed in 2016. This man had been a pillar in his community, yet only a private memorial was held.

Perhaps my brother Michael best summed up our fortuitous meeting in a letter to me when he declared, "Please thank your mother for so graciously enabling you to go on this journey to find us. Finding each other is only about addition, never subtraction."

CHAPTER 25

Birthday of Birthdays and Beyond

In June 1997, I traveled with my family to Monterey for a family birthday party—the one we had never had! This time, my brother from back east came along with his wife and three children as well, and Michael's son was also in attendance. We checked Kathleen out of her nursing home for the afternoon and went to a park surrounded by redwoods. The trees were so tall that they provided a sort of filtering of the light that was magical. To this festive event, we brought steaks to cook, green salad and fruit salad, rolls, and two large birthday cakes. My husband readied the fire to cook the meat, and we all visited, getting to know each other better and enjoying each other's company.

After our delicious meal, I pulled out five gifts that I had purchased and wrapped for my brothers. Even though two of them did not have June birthdays, they all received gifts for all their birthdays I had missed through the years. I had gotten them watches, all different and what I felt suited their personalities. My brother from New York, the one born just after me, gave me a beautiful picture of a forest scene with deer achieved by cutting out wood of various trees and shades. My fourth brother presented me with a lovely gold crucifix. I also received many hugs and kisses that day. We had a joyous celebration and especially enjoyed Kathleen's countenance, which radiated love and contentment at last.

We had one day left before our trip back home, which added a bonus get-together to top off our weekend. My husband and youngest son had gone out on a salmon boat early in the morning and came back with the catch of the day. Fifteen salmon were gutted, cut, and otherwise prepared for a fish fry at Lovers Point. We called all to meet us there, where we grilled the fish and fresh corn on the cob and ate soft, chewy sourdough bread slathered with sweet, creamy butter. It was a feast of feasts and so appropriate to be held at the place that Kathleen loved the best—a place that I had often visited while in utero.

It has been twenty-one years since we were all together. Several times, I went back to Monterey to visit Mother Kathleen and whichever brothers could meet at our pizza place. On one trip, we found her out on the patio of her care facility with her boyfriend; they were both in their wheelchairs, sitting side by side and holding hands, each wearing a hat to keep the sun from their faces. Laughing and smiling at each other, they didn't even notice our approach. Of course, it wasn't long before he passed away, and she was left alone again.

On another trip, she was hungry for a big hamburger, so Michael bought Whoppers and all ate them together on the patio. Oh, did she enjoy that hamburger! Juice from it just ran down her hand and arm! She always wanted a Diet Coke when we visited, and my husband always accommodated her by making a trip to the soda machine. He always left her money for several more when we departed. Funny that she never asked us for cigarettes or money to buy them. Other family members commented that she always asked them for some when they visited.

Every year after I found her, I sent Christmas, birthday, and Mother's Day gifts, and cards, candy, and flowers for all the other holidays. For the first Christmas after I found her, I sent her an album of pictures of me from babyhood up to high school graduation. Each time we visited, I noticed that she always kept that close on her bedside table.

My youngest brother has come to Las Vegas twice and met us for dinner, and he is the only one who ever got to meet my mom, Thelma. My New York brother came once and met us for a meal. We also visited him at his home once and attended a Yankees game with his family. I have treasured these times and cherished these memories. Our youngest daughter and her family visited Kathleen once, and her little girls entertained Kathleen with their singing and dancing. Our youngest son traveled down to see her on a summer road trip and greatly enjoyed his conversation with her at that time.

My mom, Thelma, passed in 2010 of Alzheimer's disease. She had lived to age ninety-one and lived twenty-one of those years without my dad. So many couples that live together as long as they did don't last long once one of them passes on. This was not the case with my mom. I have no doubt that she lived on to watch over me, her precious daughter, and the jewels, her four delightful grandchildren, I had given her.

The summer after my mother passed away, we went down to see Mother Kathleen, not knowing at the time that it would be our last visit. We stopped at a florist shop along the way to buy her a bouquet of flowers to enjoy. Upon reaching her room, we found she was distressed and didn't want to see us; she actually told us to leave. I started crying, but my youngest son wasn't going to have that. He spoke up: "Kathleen, this is your daughter! She has traveled all the way from Las Vegas to see you. I am your grandson. Do you remember that I came to visit you a few summers ago?"

After he told her these things to jog her memory, she questioned,

"My daughter? You're my daughter?" Clearly, she was suffering from the effects of dementia. We stayed with her only a short time that day until she fell asleep.

Mother Kathleen died at the age of eighty-five, just one year after my mom and of the same disease. Coincidence? I think not. If I have learned anything through this journey, it is that nothing was coincidence—it was all meant to be. At her passing, my five brothers, my husband, and I met one last time on a bench at Lovers Point to discuss our mother's arrangements—so appropriate that we should meet there on her favorite stretch of beach! We then traveled to the funeral home to say our last good-byes in the chapel of the same facility. At first, we all gathered around the coffin to look at her peaceful countenance. Michael commented that he had never seen her look so peaceful. Then, one by one, we had our individual time to tell her what was in our hearts.

Her struggle was finally over. No one will ever know the extent of her battle with this existence that we call *mortality*, so many years alone with her troubled mind, but there is one thing of which I'm certain: she loved more fiercely than anyone I've ever known besides my mother who raised me.

CHAPTER 26

Where Does the Story End?

My adoption story does not have a storybook ending. I have struggled with having two families. My adoptive parents had taught me loyalty and allegiance, and when my mom began to struggle with the time I spent with my birth family, I had to pull back. I needed to spend her last five years with her only, helping her navigate the illness that was robbing her of her mind and identity. That was my place. Mother Kathleen had chosen that for me.

I'm sorry that I couldn't have been more to my birth mother. I think that she wanted me to save her from the life she was living, but I didn't know how to do that. I already had a mother who needed my care, and I couldn't do more than I was doing. I'm sorry that I didn't have the capacity to stretch that far.

I am not sorry, however, that I found my birth family. I have five amazing brothers who have done incredibly well with the cards that life dealt them. Life is hard, but theirs has been harder than those of many. We have a bond that goes beyond sharing the same blood and DNA. That bond is the gift of a mother who chose to give us life and to do the best that she could for each of us under the circumstances in which we were born. For that, I will be ever grateful.

EPILOGUE

What will this story mean to my readers? I desire that they will find it a story of hope, that it will be a guide to a quest that they may be living through. To those who were adopted and are searching for the missing pieces to make them whole and complete, may they follow their hearts, embrace the love that is theirs to find, and hold tight to the life and identity that their blessed adoptive parents have provided for them. They have been given a gift, a divine gift, one to cherish and treasure forever.

To those who have made the ultimate sacrifice of placing a child up for adoption, may they know that at some time in their lives, they will be blessed for their determination and unselfishness. They have given their children the greatest gift of love by providing them with the opportunity to have a better life than they may have been able to supply. May they be blessed for giving other loving couples the chance to become adoring parents to their offspring.

Finally, to those who find themselves expecting a child and currently wrestling with the decision of what to do, may they not take their God-given ability too lightly; may they deeply consider all the options, knowing that they will live with their decision for the rest of their lives. Times are extremely different than they were in the 1950s when Kathleen was expecting me. Women have many more options when dealing with an unwanted pregnancy, but do they really? It might seem easier or more convenient to do away with the problem today, but in terms of the actions' results, I wonder. I am grateful that Kathleen had the presence of mind to let me live.

ABOUT THE AUTHOR

Suzanne H. Fabbi is a retired secondary English teacher, having taught for twenty-four years in middle and high school and at the college level. She is the mother of four children and grandmother to seven, and she resides with her husband and Yorkie pup in Las Vegas, Nevada.